Dedication

This book is dedicated to the founders of this fantastic organization—the late David Wimberly and the incomparable Earl A. Pace, Jr. But also to all of the BDPA family and supporters who have given their precious time and intellectual perspiration to fulfill a collective mission. Peace and love to everyone.

The BDPA Story

How
African American
Computer Technology Professionals
Changed the World

Norman R. Mays ▪ Kenneth L. Wilson ▪ Earl A. Pace, Jr.

Planet Victorious Publishing
Cleveland, Ohio

Planet Victorious Publishing, Cleveland, Oho 44118

The BDPA Story. Norman R. Mays; Kenneth L. Wilson; Earl A. Pace, Jr. -- 1st ed.
ISBN 978-0-578-33080-8

In Memory Of

National Presidents, Co-Founder, and Directors
Resting in Peace

David Wimberly
Co-Founder, BDPA

Gerard Anderson
National President

Ollie Morgan
National President
Chicago Chapter President

Diane Davis
National President
Detroit Chapter President

Vivian C. Wilson
National President
National Conference Coordinator

R. Wayne Hicks
National President
Cincinnati Chapter President
Executive Director BETF

Dr. William F. Bundy
Commander, U.S. Navy (Retired)
Outside Director and Founder, BDPA I.T. Institute

Acknowledgements

Writing a book that covers more than 45 years of organizational memories in a rapidly changing information-technology industry is a Herculean task that could not have been accomplished without the assistance of some amazing people we must acknowledge here.

First and foremost, we thank each and every BDPA member across America, and we thank all past and current, local and national officers for making our mission possible.

We thank each and every BDPA corporate supporter, past and present, who donated their time, talent, and resources backing our efforts to improve the lives of our members, our supporters, and our communities.

We thank Mr. Ralph Gordon, Ms. Wendy Wonsley, Mr. George Williams, and those who assisted in compiling a record of BDPA events from 1975 to 2000.

And a huge "thank you" goes to Mr. Gregory L. Moore, Editor in Chief of Deke Expert News, for editing, advising, and enhancing our writing and manuscript development process.

We appreciate all that you have done, and to each and every one of you, we give our most heartfelt "Thank you."

The Authors

Contents

About The Authors

Norman R. Mays grew up in Cleveland, Ohio and is the father of three sons - Prentice, Jonathan (deceased) and Christopher R. Mays. As an officer, having served two tours of duty in Vietnam in military intelligence, he was offered the opportunity to participate in the specialty field of data processing, and was subsequently, introduced to BDPA.

Earl A. Pace, Jr., grew up in Philadelphia, PA, and enjoys his large family throughout the area. A graduate of Pennsylvania State University, Earl is a successful entrepreneur who in the early 1970s started and still owns PACE Data Systems, a successful information technology business in Philadelphia. Earl is a Co-founder of BDPA.

Kenneth L. Wilson, a Cleveland native and father of four, is a technology entrepreneur with more than 40 years of experience helping people build thriving businesses. A graduate of Ohio Wesleyan University, he started out as a medical major before falling in love with computers. He founded his first company, Wilco Information Management in 1984. And in 1980, he was a founding member of the BDPA in Cleveland.

FOREWORD

Over the course of four decades, BDPA has been the pathfinder for African Americans seeking careers in the ever-changing world of data processing, then computer programming, then IT, and now STEM, Cyber and Artificial Intelligence. In this important record for future generations, Norman Mays, Kenneth Wilson, and Earl Pace capture BDPA's challenges and victories. The organization's servant-leaders have changed the professional trajectories for thousands of African Americans in the world of technology and in the process, changed our world for the better.

—David L. Steward

Founder and Chairman
World Wide Technology

PREFACE

The Story Before "The National Story"

As we embark upon telling the story of BDPA, I feel that it is imperative that you, the reader, get an understanding of why this book was written. The reasons **why** I stood up during the Awards Ceremony Dinner at one of our national conferences and announced to the audience—to the world—that Earl A. Pace, Jr. and I were going to write a book about BDPA and its history—The reasons are, I did not want someone else—who doesn't come from where we come from—attempting to tell our story. Plus, I realized that there was only a short period of time to "collect" the story: That period of time is while the participants in the story are still "with us." Thankfully, the project moved "full speed ahead," when Kenneth L. Wilson, already a published author, joined our team and proposed an accelerated approach.

Our Story is Unique

Many professional organizations don't have as long, as enduring, and as impactful a life as the BDPA organization. We have been helping IT Professionals and Communities for more than 45 years. Our story is too personal, too unique, and too inspiring for someone other than a person who has lived it to try to tell it.

Building a National Organization

Upon realizing that a national organizational approach would be the best way for introducing African-Americans to the field of data processing, BDPA National was started. We knew that if we wanted to grow chapters rapidly and unify across the country, we would have to promote sharing. In BDPA, it's okay to copy, duplicate, and replicate what works well. If it works well in one chapter, we make it available for every chapter to customize it locally. For structure, we utilize "Robert's Rules of Order" because they are "tried and true" and easily duplicatable.

Labor of Love

For me, the effort in building the national organization was a labor of love and an unforgettable bonding experience. Aside from the fond memories of deep philosophical discussions, debates and friendly arguments about, "Why this? What about that? What if we did this?," and the subsequent teasing, there was breakfast at IHOP or at Earl's mother's house when in Philly. One 9AM morning in Philly, while sitting around the kitchen table, we started pouring out ideas, "We could do this, we could do that." We went back and forth, until we came to an agreement on a particular point or concept.

The energy we generated from brainstorming would invariably lead to teasing and cajoling in ways that only best friends can. Many times, one of us would laugh so hard that our stomachs would cramp as we're on the floor in tears from laughing. Then it was back to business and the cycle would start all over again.

Here is an example of how our "teasing and trash talking" led to an extended—yet temporary—period of insanity. During one of our work sessions in Philly, the subject of "one's basketball prowess" came up and we ended up on a nearby outdoor basketball court. This is where insanity really set in. The kicker was: We were dressed in regular dress shoes, shirts and dress slacks. The humidity was high and the temperature was in the high 90 degrees. Plus, there was no shade. Now visualize this: Four ill prepared, out of shape, fast-becoming-middle-aged "dudes," sweating like mad men, and trying to play like the superstar Dr. "J." WOW! When we finished, our feet were killing us, we were rank, and even though Earl played "slightly" better than the rest of us (trash talking continues), we had one hell of a good time! That's just one part of what I mean when I said, one had to have lived it to capture and share that feeling. That's BDPA!

The results of our "sweat" were the creation of working documents that would be adopted as BDPA's National Bylaws, and Guidelines for BDPA's National Structure. And in 1979, our tireless efforts led to the formation of a National BDPA, and our first "National BDPA Conference," which was convened in Washington D.C.

Earl Pace, Wilbur McReynolds, Ralph Gordon, Norman Mays

That same year, in 1979, after 20 years of service in the U.S. Army, I returned to my hometown Cleveland, Ohio. The following year, in March of 1980, I founded the third chapter of BDPA. The national vision had truly begun.

— Norman R. Mays

INTRODUCTION

This book was written to enrich your life. It is a story about helping people grow, build, and achieve greatness. The story of the Black Data Processing Associates (BDPA) — a non-profit organization of African-American computer technology professionals growing, building, and achieving success together — is one of developing diverse talent and improving their career options in the Information Technology industry.

Earl A. Pace, Jr., BDPA Founder, Norman R. Mays, the innovative mover-and-shaker who put the BDPA onto the path to become a national organization, and Kenneth L. Wilson, the first founding member of the Cleveland chapter, wrote this book to memorialize the history of this groundbreaking organization. Collectively, we have served this organization for more than a century. It has been worth it.

An organization of tech professionals, BDPA has been a home away from home, and a family away from family. We have always known that Black Lives Matter. And BDPA continues to inspire us to be as useful and productive as we possibly can be.

BDPA was born in 1975 because its founders believed African Americans in particular were marginalized in the burgeoning field of data processing, later known as information technology. Before BDPA, African Americans had been ignored, rejected, segregated, or pushed to the back of the employment line. From a series of events experienced by co-founder, Earl A. Pace, Jr., the BDPA story begins.

Earl worked as a vice-president and data processing consultant for a group of banks in Philadelphia. In his professional capacity, Earl attended dozens of data-processing seminars and symposiums. But disappointingly, Earl was almost always the only African-American professional in attendance. And because of the tan color of Earl's skin, he was often excluded from conversations with other attendees, or his questions were met with vague or condescending answers — or no answers at all.

To fully understand Earl's predicament, recall the exclusionary corporate culture that was common prior to 1975. Yes, 21st-Century racism continues to exist in many aspects of our society, but it was really, really, really bad back then. Also, these same corporations were both the primary users of data processing, and the primary convener of data processing seminars and symposiums Earl was attending. America—back then—was fresh from the daily headlines of the Civil Rights Movement, and American companies were struggling to accept and include a diverse workforce.

Back then, Information Technology (IT) was still being called “Data Processing.” According to Wikipedia, the word "data" was first used in 1946 to mean "transmissible and storable computer information." The expression "data processing" was first used in 1954. Also, the term “Information Technology” first came into common usage during the late 1970s—and it remains in common usage today.

During the decade leading up to 1975, a computer-usage revolution—the likes of which corporations could not have possibly imagined—blasted off into the stratosphere. New innovations were being announced daily. Those innovations included: The COBOL business-programming language, IBM mainframes (IBM 360 and 370), the DEC PDP 8 Mini-Computer, Computer Timesharing Systems, Local Area Networks, Networked Email, The “C” Programming Language, and Precursors to the Internet.

A new business-technology paradigm shift was underway, shaking up the workplace and changing forever how every business would operate.

Moreover, as corporate computer usage skyrocketed, the corporate need and demand for computer programmers, analysts, operators, and managers also skyrocketed.

Inspired by the aforementioned business, societal and technological opportunities, Earl Pace, and his co-worker—the late David Wimberly—sat down together and conceived the Black Data Processing Associates. They realized that the expansion of computer technology brought with it an opportunity for African Americans to obtain skills and career advancement beyond data-entry positions.

Earl and David had many discussions and debates about how to address this need. David, a programmer analyst, was concerned with the lack of career mobility of minorities, and the lucrative minority placement services dominated by non-minorities. Earl was more focused on the lack of minorities in middle and upper management, and the poor preparation of minorities for these positions. Sadly along the way, David Wimberly passed away. But, after a period of mourning, Earl got back to work.

Earl decided that a community-focused organizational approach would be best; one that would:

- Introduce African Americans to the field of data processing;

- Facilitate and champion their success;

- Be a community-focused non-profit organization—as opposed to a for-profit corporate entity.

Thereupon, the conceptual framework for BDPA was born.

From BDPA's founding in 1975 to today, tens of thousands of hard-working people of color have contributed to BDPA's success. It takes a village to build an organization like this. But this book focuses on 15 pioneers and innovators chiefly responsible for BDPA's growth and success during its formative years.

This book is a collection of biographies, a chapter for each selected member, not a chronological recitation of historical events. You may also notice that we focused mainly on members from Philadelphia, Washington, D.C., and Cleveland — the first three BDPA Chapter cities. We emphasized these cities because the national blueprint for BDPA was built around these three cities. It is our expectation that future books about BDPA will focus on many more of our amazing members from the 50+ BDPA chapters across the country. Clearly, BDPA as we know it today would not exist without chapters in Chicago, Detroit, Atlanta, and more.

For some readers, this book may be a roadmap for becoming a successful entrepreneur. For others, it may be a handbook for building a successful career. For leaders of business, government, and non-profit groups, this book may be a how-to-manual for helping people overcome systemic obstacles and achieve organizational aims. As you begin this adventure, our hope is you shall seek, find, and live eternal success.

— The Authors

Part I

How BDPA Was Born

Earl A. Pace, Jr.

CHAPTER 1

Earl A. Pace, Jr.

Earl Pace, Jr. is an entrepreneur, business owner, and information technology industry activist. He is President and CEO of Pace Data Systems, a full service information technology company concentrating on banks, credit unions, state, and municipal government agencies. A native of Philadelphia, Pennsylvania, and a graduate of the Pennsylvania State University, Earl co-founded the Black Data Processing Associates organization, where he organized the first chapter, served as its first President, and served as its first National President. Most outstandingly, Earl is a member of the CompTIA I.T. Hall of Fame, along with Steve Jobs, Michael Dell, and Bill Gates.

In a January 19, 2021, recorded interview, Earl Pace talked about his career, his life and BDPA.

Searching for Simpatico

By Earl A. Pace, Jr.

I graduated with a degree in Personnel and Labor Relations, under the business school. My intent was to go to law school and become a Labor Arbitrator. This was in the mid-1960s, and the Vietnam War was going on, and particularly in Philadelphia, which is a big union town, the transportation people would go on strike, the railroad employees would go on strike for more pay and different working conditions. Very often, it would end up in court, sometimes in federal labor arbitration courts where they would be represented by attorneys. And I thought it would be a nice career to become one of those lawyers.

I was married then, and we had a child in my last year of college. And I had an uncle-in-law who was employed at the Pennsylvania Railroad and he managed to secure an interview for me during my senior year at Penn State. This was when affirmative action was in its high point in America. So, during my interview, which went well, the interviewer said to me, "Well, you know what? We would like to make you an offer. However, we don't have any openings in Labor Relations, but we do have some openings in the new area that we are forming, the Computer Programming area. And we have an internal training program for people who enter that new project for us."

Now in college I had one systems course, and we didn't touch a computer, okay? The difference was that this new area at the Pennsylvania Railroad paid more than the position in the labor relations side. A little bit more money was attractive. I could always go to law school at night if I wanted to. So, I accepted the position, and never looked back.

Pennsylvania Railroad trained me. We were programming on IBM 1401 Computers, with 4000 positions of core, in something called SPS, Standard Symbolic Programming systems, where you had to know how fast the disks were spinning, and how much core. You had to really know that machine. And it was quite a technical feat to be able to write a program. So that's how I got into computer programming. And I never looked back.

Two years later, there was an Operations Research department opening at the Pennsylvania Railroad. But my manager's manager would not let me go. So I started looking around to see what I was worth in the market because I wasn't going to let him stymie my career.

Online Service Corporation

I interviewed with a small company that was being formed by nine community savings banks in the Philadelphia area. The banks formed this co-op and they needed their own data center because most of them were being serviced by commercial banks at that time.

But the community banks were second class citizens paying first class money. And I thought the co-op was a good idea.

I didn't know anything about banking, but I knew how to program a computer, and they hired what they called their "Four Computer Lions," myself and three other people. At night, the Presidents of the banks would come down and teach us banking. During the day, we would be designing this new system, and we ended up developing one of the first online-real-time financial processing systems in the country. And it took us about two years to fully develop this system. Then we started converting banks. So that was what I would call the beginning of the Fintech area, 1967-69.

While I was at Online Service Corporation I became a Programming Manager, and eventually moved into a Vice President's position, where myself and one other fellow ended up reporting to the board. I had the marketing and technical-development side, and he had the communications side. By that point in time, the two of us were basically running the company that had grown from servicing the original nine owners to, when I left it in 1976, we had 58 banks.

There's a lot of stories in between there, but that was the genesis of some meetings and seminars that I went to that showed me that BDPA was needed for the market that existed in 1975.

The Seminar in Arizona

I went to a seminar in Mountain Shadows, Arizona. And the seminar was on something called Basic Telecommunications Access Method (BTAM), which even sounds formidable, but it was the communications platform that our online-real-time core bank processing system operated on. And it was some pretty heavy stuff that was covered in the seminar.

It was about 200 people who were at the Programming-Manager-or-above level that attended the seminar. I was, literally, "the fly in the bowl of milk."

I had been a basketball player in high school, and played a little basketball while I was at Penn State. I'm about six-five. During the seminar when there was a break, I'd mingle with the other attendees to talk about some of the concepts that we were studying. But whenever I would join the informal conversations, it would invariably turn to basketball, and that was not my interest.

So, as I looked around the room, I said, “Who can I talk to that I would have some simpatico with?” But it wasn’t there. And that prejudgment of me convinced me that there was a need for Black Data Processing Associates.

IT “Headhunters” Recruiters

Now, in those days, the supply of computer programmers and people who knew what is now "IT" was woefully inadequate, but the demand was just outrageous.

I would get, David Wimberly would get, and I'm sure most of our peers would get four to five calls a week from a headhunter who had a position that paid more than we were making.

Now, most people nowadays buy QuickBooks off the shelf for four or five hundred dollars, and they can run a company on QuickBooks. But in 1975, if you knew Accounts Receivable, Accounts Payable and General Ledger, and knew how to program them for companies, you were in high demand. So you'd get a call, and they'd say, "Hey Earl, I have this 'Company A' over here who needs somebody in your receivables payables and general ledger, and it pays X thousand dollars a year more than you're making now."

And too many of our peers would accept positions of that nature and make a move for a year, maybe two. And then you'd get another call, sometimes from the same headhunter. So very often people would make a move and get one year of experience, and they would find themselves in the position where they had these what's called "golden handcuffs," where they were making a lot of money but instead of being in a big management or creative position, they were still a programmer analyst, making nice money.

Ever-changing Technologies

All of us knew that things like QuickBooks were on the way.

And the same was happening with computer programming. Once we got COBOL, you didn't need to know machine language anymore, because COBOL let you use English to program a computer. But today, COBOL is an ancient language.

When I returned from that seminar in Mountain Shadows, Arizona, my interactions with David Wimberly intensified. We worked in the same building, and David had been pressing me to start an organization like BDPA, even though for different reasons.

It's almost as though David Wimberly had my administrative assistant on the payroll, because every time I would leave my office to go down the hall to the men's room, it seemed that David Wimberly was there, ready to say something. And his conversation would invariably come around to his thought that we should start something. He was a computer programmer also. This was 1974-75. Finally, I said, "Yeah, I think it's something we ought to do." We had some lunch meetings, and discovered that we both wanted to do it, but we wanted to do it for different reasons.

David Wimberly was more interested in accumulating a network of data processing people—programmers in particular—because of the four to five calls people were getting every week with positions. He wanted to start something that was similar to a headhunter organization, where you would attract the programmers and then be able to refer programming type people either to headhunters or to companies.

My interest was in accumulating the expertise, and letting people, who were in the industry already, enter an inner circle of knowledge and learn how to control their own positions for career advancement. And because the industry was obviously growing by leaps and bounds—growth created by abundant demand and lack of supply— here was an opportunity for people who were not in the industry to learn about it. And on top of all of that, this organization would open up opportunities for students, and mothers and fathers of young people who were still in college, high school, and junior high school, too.

Most people didn't know about this industry and back then, you didn't have to have a college degree to be a programmer. You could get a job as a tape handler in a data processing organization and be in the computer room loading tapes. Then if you operated in the proper way on your job, interfacing with the other I.T. people, volunteering to work on the United Way campaign, going to community college, doing the right things that you need to do in an organization, you can move up, from a keypunch operator or tape handler to somebody who was a computer operator now, who is loading all the cards in the machine, asking questions of the programmers, and taking some of the training courses that the companies were offering.

Ralph Gordon, who I'm sure you'll hear about later, operated what he called his SWAT team at an insurance company where he had 15 to 20 people in training programs that he controlled. So the companies were training people themselves. But some mothers and fathers didn't know about that, and I thought we could reach out to them.

So we put our money together and we started BDPA. Each of us went into our pockets, David Wimberly, and me. I think it was maybe $30 for me and $30 from him. And we rented a hotel room at the Philadelphia Sheraton Hotel, and just by word of mouth started talking to some of our friends about a meeting that we were calling and set the date.

Showed up at the meeting, and sure enough, there's 15, 20 people ready to talk about the organization. Howard James, Ralph Gordon, Craig Bethea, Doug Funderburg, Mary Ann Lowry, Roy Barnes, David Benson, and Charles Jones. These are all people who showed up and said, "Yeah, this makes sense." So that was a start.

Then tragically, suddenly, David Wimberly passed away. And also tragically, to this day, we do not know the specifics of what happened. But we did know that we had to move on. And part of that moving on—and rightfully so—is that David Wimberly is and will always be honored as a Co-Founder of BDPA.

Pace Data Systems

If you look at the dates, you'll find that we started BDPA in 1975, May, June, July, in that area. And I started Pace Data Systems in 1976, one year after.

Well, those are pretty parallel issues, both driven by an obvious need, an opportunity, and an entrepreneurial mindset.

Looking back on my life, I've almost never been without a job. On my first job—at 11 or 12—I was working in a grocery store, stocking shelves, and making deliveries. Then I became a paper boy, and while I had those jobs, I sold fire extinguishers from door to door.

In 1955-56, the city was tearing down the South Philadelphia public-housing shipyard homes, where we lived, and they had announced they were going to relocate everybody. Well, my mother—who was a natural entrepreneur herself—and my stepfather did not like the area that they were planning to move us to, so we all put our money together and bought a house out in what's called West Philadelphia.

And they bought this house because it had a storefront. And one of the first things we did with that storefront is convert it into a dry cleaners. Then my mother quit her job and started operating this dry cleaners full time. And guess who became her assistant? I would come home from school, or basketball practice, and work in that dry cleaners; making deliveries, learning how to press clothes, and doing things of that nature.

During the Christmas season, I would take the little money I had, buy Christmas trees, line them up in front of the dry cleaners, and sell them. Simply stated, I became an entrepreneur at an early age.

And having an entrepreneurial mindset made me more comfortable going to Online Service Corporation. When it became obvious to me that I had outgrown Online Service Corporation, I launched Pace Data Systems.

Launching Pace Data Systems

There was a shakeup at Online Service Corporation. The fellow who hired us; we were very loyal to him. We found out that in spite of all that we had changed there, the Christmas bonuses and the increases that were being given out were not proportionate to the effort that we had been expending. So, there was a disgruntled kind of attitude amongst the programmers. And at that time, I was the programming manager.

The board decided to shake up the administration, and they let that president go. But before they let that president go, they spoke to me and to Bronus Desupinsky, who was the fellow who was on the other side who did the savings and communications, to find out if they let that president go, would we also go because they thought we were so loyal to him that if they got rid of him, that we'd walk also.

Well, I wasn't about to give my job up for somebody because they had run afoul of the board. So when they found out that all of us would not leave, they let him go, and they promoted myself and Desupinsky to Vice

President positions, with Bronus inside, keeping the communications going; and having me take marketing; and since I would be interfacing with all the customers, I would maintain responsibility for the technical development side.

So, I put together marketing budgets and it went fine. We kept growing, adding banks and everything. Everything was great. We were growing fine.

But our customers had some demands, and they were big. The equipment they wanted was hard to get. So I was able to get a new company that was developing a new version of the same kind of tele-terminals that were being used in our other banks with some additional capabilities. I also, since I had developed the mortgage side, I was able to do some tweaks to our mortgage processing for them to do some of the things that they wanted.

And they also wanted a couple of programmers that would be hired, not hired by them, but paid by them and work for online service that would make sure that some of the things that they wanted to get done got done. I didn't see any problem with that. And so we did, and we ran them in a parallel basis. They had converted all of their large dollar loans (they call them jumbo loans) over to our system and processed them for about a year, so they could find out if it would work fine.

And it did, and they were ready to sign a contract. And that contract would have represented my quota for the entire year. I took the contract to the board, and the board said, "No, no, we don't want them because they're so big and so powerful, they're going to be paying for two programmers themselves. Pretty soon, they're going to be controlling Online Service Corporation." So, they would not sign the contract, and I had to go back to this customer, that we had on the hook for that long, and tell them that the board wouldn't go for it. They were incensed, and so was I. So I knew that at that point in time I had outgrown that company.

So, I had been attending DPMA meetings. That's where the “movers and shakers” were. They poured some good drinks at those meetings, too. But you got a chance to mingle with people who were business owners.

And at one of those meetings I met Eartha and Henry Lipmanson. She was African-American, and he was Jewish, and they ran a company called Superior Keypunching Service. And I got to know them over a two-year period. I'd see him at all the DPMA meetings, and we’d have discussions. But when I got this big disappointment at Online Service Corporation, I had started having a little different conversation with them, and they were ready to retire. And back then companies were still using computer cards, IBM 5081 punch cards. The Lipmansons had a decent punch-card-based business.

And with my entrepreneurial bent, I started thinking, "Did I want to continue as an employee at a company where the board would turn down (business) after a year and a half, two years' worth of courting a customer?" And the answer was no. So in my conversations with the Lipmansons, they said, "Well, you know, we're thinking of retiring." I said, "Would you ever think about selling your business?" They said, "Yeah, you interested?" And I said, "I might be."

So I ended up taking out a small business loan, putting my house up as collateral, and striking a purchasing deal with the Lipmansons to buy their company. I thought—erroneously—that the same people who would be calling me about mortgage processing, as a result of being an Online Service Corporation officer, would call me as President of Pace Data Systems. Wrong!

I left Online Service Corporation on December 31, 1976, and became president of Superior Keypunching Service (trading as Pace Data Systems) on January 1, 1977. I hung out my shingle and waited for the first call. I'm still waiting for it. It was fine for me to get these calls when I was working for somebody else. But when I became the owner of it, and wanted to talk about contracts for doing it, it was different.

There were still five or six banks that did come to me because I had an independent company that could process them as they were moving from savings accounts into checking accounts. They were called NOW accounts. So, Pace Data Systems used to do the initial processing for them because we were a little more flexible. We used to send work from a credit union or a bank, convert their NOW account into checking transactions, overnight them up to State Street in Boston. They would get the reports back, and they would be operating these NOW accounts, which were like checking accounts, because checking accounts were not legal for thrift industry. And we did that until mega corporations like EDS and Boeing Computer Systems saw it as a growing industry, and they snatched that business away.

So I found myself operating a company that had some business on the keypunch side, and some government contracts. But needed to change the business.

My vision was that I would use my IT knowledge to move from keypunch to key-to-tape, and I started getting other types of contracts, and became a government SBA 8(a) company for a while until President Ronald Reagan came in and told us all we had to get out of the program. So that's another story altogether.

Reflections

Has BDPA been all I dreamed it would be?

Well, I think we could have done more. When we started BDPA it was because the industry, the computer industry, the data processing industry, in 1975 held significant possibilities. I used to compare it to television repair. In 1975 or earlier, when you bought a television, and it started "going on the blink," you called a TV repairman. Nowadays, you simply throw the TV out, and you go get another one, because they're less expensive.

And as the industry grew, some black brothers, and sisters learned how to repair televisions. And when my family called to get a TV repair, it was a black guy that came to fix that TV set for us. And they weren't engineers. They didn't go to college and learn how to repair TVs. They went to a TV repair school, and they learned how to fix those TVs.

Likewise, in the data-processing industry in 1975, there was this phenomenal demand for personnel; a career that did not necessitate having a college degree. And if you're raising soon-to-be-on-their-own teenagers, you now knew about an area that's paying good money, where that young person could move into and do very well.

So, data processing was an opportunity for the African-American community. And that industry did not have enough people and would not have enough people to satisfy the demand, for years and years and years. So here was this great big opportunity sitting there that most people in the black community didn't know about. But here was an organization (BDPA) that had some people who were in it, and could demonstrate to the black community what they've done and say, "You can do it too!"

And it's no different today. Here we are in 2021, and we don't have enough supply to meet the demand for

IT personnel. The industry didn't just go through that normal stage of new development, maturation, then decline. It's almost as though the curve of development for the computer industry just kept going up, up, up, up, up, and we haven't reached the end of it. Okay?

So can you imagine that if the vision for BDPA of being influential within this industry had been realized? And again, I'm looking at it as a founder. My view is that BDPA is the promise unfulfilled. It has not done what I envisioned it would do.

I envisioned an IT industry where there would be a significant African-American influence. In 1975, if more of us had moved up and into this IT industry, there would be more businesses, more wealth, and more resources flowing back into the community.

And I take Pace Data Systems as an example. Pace Data Systems, has not grown as much as it could or should have. Pace Data Systems, operating under Superior Keypunch, had helped dozens of banks develop their online-real-time processing. But the vast majority of those customers I called on at Online Service Corporation did not do business with me at Pace Data Systems. And later I found out that because of my leadership position in BDPA—the Black Data Processing Associates—and because I wanted to, needed to talk about the racism that existed in the IT industry; I found out that banking presidents didn't like my speaking out. Some of them wished I would shut up about racism, and just be CEO of Pace Data Systems.

Had BDPA been able to satisfy the demand, and we had more African-American owned businesses, and if those businesses could have done business with other African American companies, then just like other racial groups of people who were more equitably represented, African Americans would have received a more equitable portion of jobs, contracts, and opportunities in the IT industry.

I wished we could have done more. But we will.

Economic Parity

To me, the end goal would be economic parity. And to me, that is where we want to get to, at least to economic parity. I think the Hispanics of color, and other minorities suffer from the same issues that the African-American does. Our contribution economically to what happens in the United States is miniscule. There are, let's say, 10,000 African-American owned businesses in the United States, but based on the percentage that we are in the population, instead of 10,000, we should have 60,000 businesses.

Instead of employing 30,000 employees, we should be employing 265,000 people. The revenue in those companies should not be $500 million, it should be $6 trillion, or something. I'm making up numbers, but if we had economic parity, and had our 12 to 13 percent of those business operations, unemployment wouldn't be a problem within the African-American community because we'd be hiring people according to our percentages. And anybody can get these reports out of the Minority Business Development Agency. So it's not that I'm so smart that I can produce these numbers; they're right here in front of us all the time. So, reflecting back from 1975 and today, the same message should be delivered: that with that economic parity, unemployment wouldn't be a problem within the African-American community.

In my opening comments for the online National Conference that BDPA had in 2020, I talked about how buoyed I was by the Black Lives Matter movement. I was uplifted because it reminded me of 1975 when we were starting BDPA. At one point in time, BDPA grew to like 65 chapters across the country. We were actually bringing in 30, 35, 40 high school computer competition teams. Our youth conference had 200, 300, 400 hundred members, nine, ten years old. So we were starting young on the classroom side and bringing up experienced people through the development side.

So when I look at the Black Lives Matter movement I see shades of what we were trying to do in 1975 — advance a people and change economic opportunity in America.

Moreover, I am buoyed that some of the purposes and reasons that BDPA was formed are having a resurgence in the United States now. We had four years of a backward slide (under President Donald Trump) that fought utilization of people and hurt people. But with our current administration in Washington, and with the Black Lives movement pushing, and with other people continuing to assist them, we can start that growth all over again. And some of the promise of change that existed in 1975 can have a resurgence, and we can move forward from here.

Ralph E. Gordon, Jr.

CHAPTER 2

Ralph E. Gordon, Jr.

Ralph Gordon is a friendly, down-to-earth, hard-working black man who started at the bottom of the tech-services industry and worked his way up to the top the old-fashioned way—by staying with it, year after year. And today, Ralph owns Gordon Consulting, while generously volunteering his time in the San Francisco Bay Area. Ralph previously worked at IBM, Oracle, and others, and excelled in Business Alliances, Sales, Enterprise Software, Partner Management, and Customer Relationship Management (CRM). Ralph was a member of the original Philadelphia team working with Earl Pace to create BDPA's original structure. Born, raised, and educated in the Philadelphia area, Ralph served BDPA in several leadership roles, including Chapter President. During a January 14, 2021, recorded interview, Ralph talked about his career, his life, and BDPA.

I'd Like to Be That Guy

By Ralph E. Gordon, Jr.

I got into the data processing world at the bottom as a clerk, but through the assistance, support, and faith, I rose through the ranks from a computer operator to computer programmer. I started out in the public sector, in the school district of Philadelphia, and moved on to jobs in private enterprise. I became an instructor of COBOL, a manager, and I ran a program to teach people how to become programmers. And I was able to hire a number of folks and bring them into the industry, and give them opportunities. And it was nice to be able to do that.

I was eventually able to get into management and was really excited about doing that. I was on the technical side supporting sales organizations. Then a dear friend of mine, who saw how competitive I was in sports, said that my "superficial genteel nature" belied the fact that I was tough underneath, and maybe I could do "the sales thing." So I got into sales, and wound up having success there.

Ultimately, I landed at Oracle Corporation, and worked there for about six years. My time at Oracle was like being in graduate school. At that time (1989-1995), Oracle was not a household name like it is today. Back then, Oracle had to battle against Sybase and other database companies. We had not yet become dominant in the industry, and we were just starting to spread out globally.

When I became a Global Account Manager, I worked with clients "on both sides of the pond," as the "Brits" like to call the Atlantic Ocean. This multicultural experience working with overseas clients was important for my progression at Oracle and growth in the information technology and services industries. My clients at Oracle were mostly in the pharmaceutical industry as biotech was just starting to come about.

I had been traveling to Oracle headquarters in California, meeting clients. We called them red carpet visits when you would bring clients to the corporate headquarters to educate and entertain them. And even prior to getting into sales and those red carpet visits, I had been traveling to offices in Los Angeles and the San Francisco Bay area as a trainer/educator, teaching clients about products, services, and technologies. During my travels, I discovered dramatic differences between the Northern and Southern regions of the huge State of California. Ultimately, the San Francisco Bay area enticed me, and in 1990, when Oracle offered me the opportunity to relocate there, I was ready to go, made the move, and I've been here ever since. I love it in the Bay area; I love the beauty; I love the diversity; those kinds of things. And the weather's not bad either.

After leaving Oracle in 1995, I moved on to more venturesome enterprises—I won't detail them all. But I survived the hard knocks of small-business startups (1995-2005). If anybody wants to wallpaper their house, I've got plenty of stock certificates from defunct startups; they'll be wet because they're all underwater.

That's why I had to go back to my "bread and butter", and ultimately in 2006, I wound up at IBM, which is interesting because I had once taught a course about IBM, but had never dreamed I'd join the IBM family.

At IBM, I worked in a sales capacity focused on financial organizations, servicing large accounts. And if you're in sales, you know there are different dynamics working with small versus large companies, and over time, I developed a fondness for working with large companies. When servicing large companies, you have fewer clients in your portfolio, but you have many more people in those organizations you have to work with. Time flew, and I ended up working 13 years at IBM, and subsequently in 2019, I retired from IBM.

Mentorship

Throughout my career, I've been blessed by people who've mentored me, like for example, back when I was a clerk at the school board making only "four figures," and dreaming of the day I'd finally make more than $10,000 a year. Back then, I'd sometimes get discouraged, but I had a mentor who kept telling me, "You can do this, and you can do that. You'll learn how to program computers, and you're not gonna stay a clerk." Admittedly, I thought the guy was crazy, but he knew what he was talking about, and he took me under his wing. And eventually, all of the things he told me I could do— in terms of a job, in terms of education, and all kinds of things—I wound up doing all of those things with the help of his encouragement.

Later, when I got involved with BDPA in Philadelphia—and we weren't even calling it BDPA yet—I saw an individual, at one of our meetings, who I thought was very, very sharp, and I thought to myself, "Man, I'd like to be like that guy. I'd like to talk to him and get some advice from this guy, and hitch my wagon to him, and see what I can do." And I thought to myself, "I know a lot a guys are going to want to get up next to him and get his advice and help, but I'll take a number and stand in line, and then maybe I can get some benefit out of this really sophisticated professional black man." Well, the intriguing thing is that when the meeting ended, there was no line. Nobody was standing there waiting to get with him—but I did. I went up and said, "Hey, my name is Ralph Gordon. I'd like to talk to you some time... just pick your brain. I'm trying to get moving forward in this career." And the guy said "yeah," and we became friends, and we've remained friends. That guy was Earl Pace.

So, when you want to go somewhere, you need to find somebody you can connect with who is willing to talk to you, help you, advise you on how to become who or what you want to become. And Earl has been a tremendous influence in my life, not only professionally, but personally in terms of how I carry myself as a black man and as a gentleman.

Launching BDPA

When Earl Pace, David Wimberly, myself, and others got together and brainstormed back in 1975-76, we knew there was a need for a BDPA type of organization. David Wimberly was the heart and soul of BDPA in terms of envisioning where this group could go and what it could be. Earl was the rock in terms of "let's do this." I understand that there are skits and dramatizations about how we got started. I haven't seen any of the skits, but I've heard that I'm one of the characters.

But the organization would not (or could not) have gone national without Norman Mays. We were just going to be a Philly group of guys and gals in the data processing business. But Norm talked about doing BDPA in Washington, D.C., expanding our thinking beyond Philly. And after a *Computer World* story brought BDPA to the attention of prospective members in other cities, we started re-writing BDPA's bylaws and rethinking our organizational structure so that we could grow nationally.

By the time we were ready to launch, we had worked hundreds of hours putting plans in place, but it was a labor of love because we knew we were doing something good and worthwhile. And we had such good feelings about each other, that the time we spent together didn't seem like work. It was a great experience.

The First Program Meetings

We were really clear our first meeting was not going to be just a social gathering — we weren't just shooting the breeze. We were working. So, don't let us talking about all the good feeling and the kumbaya take away from the fact that we were trying to create something significant. We were on a mission. We knew that we were fighting to be allowed to participate in job opportunities that were expanding at the speed of light. And as ludicrous as it may sound today, African Americans were characterized as incapable of comprehending technology as if we were somehow less than, as if we were somehow unteachable. If the whole truth be told, some folks in the IT industry simply did not want us living in their neighborhoods. So, we were meeting to strategize how to tactfully and diplomatically convince folks in the IT industry that black people are smart, hard-working, and capable. In that regard, it was civil rights all over again.

Just as important, we were organizing and planning programs that would teach us and prepare us to be ready for any and all opportunities that might come our way. And we helped each other advance, while also encouraging others to get into this booming industry so that they could benefit like we were starting to do.

We let people know that they could become programmers, and systems analysts. But in order to help people do that we had to have an operational structure in place. And to make that happen, we needed to meet.

So we set up these monthly program meetings, and we decided that the way to attract people to these meetings we needed some kind of hook for people who had no idea what we were offering. We couldn't just say, "We gonna meet next month y'all—show up!" We had to be able to say, "Because, when you do show up, we're going to talk about how to get a good paying job as a COBOL programmer, and if you're interested in learning COBOL programming, you need to know about the four divisions of a COBOL program. And we're going to talk about how having COBOL skills (can accelerate your career). We're going to talk about why you need to know about different languages of programming, or what is important for a data processing department, or what are some of the other positions in a data processing department, or what are some careers you can aspire to. And we did all of that.

We began electing officers. We weren't haphazard about anything we were doing, so, whether we were having pancakes in Earl's mother's kitchen (planning BDPA), or whether we were having the early organizing meetings in the UCE building, we knew we were working to build a sustainable organizational foundation.

As we were deciding on a name, there were some who didn't think we should have the word "Black" as part of our name. And look at where we are right now (in the year 2021). If you say, "Black Lives Matter," think about what that does with certain folks in this population today, in terms of polarization. But it is important to say that because black lives have obviously not mattered, in terms of how we have been treated, particularly with police violence. But I said, "We *are* Black, so of course we should call ourselves Black Data Processing Associates." And "Black" has endured. Yeah, we used to be "colored," we used to be "negroes," but one thing is for sure; we are black, and black is what we have in common.

Each One, Help One

If I were speaking at a BDPA Program Meeting, I would feed off what Norman Mays said about "the moral responsibility" of BDPA, in terms of its purpose. It's not just us sitting around and beating on our chests and talking about how great we've done. Instead, our moral responsibility is actually about helping somebody else. We know the African proverb, "Each one, teach one." I believe in "Each one, help one."

I mentioned mentors who helped me, and I used to give a presentation about mentoring. Even today, I'm still mentoring, despite being semi-retired, because I have a responsibility to try to help somebody else. And the funny thing is: As I'm helping them, I'm helping myself because the questions they hit me with keep me sharp.

When we're talking about "cloud technologies," and this and that, they're keeping me on my toes. My proteges and I are talking about sales strategies, which I have a lot of experience with. And from a growth standpoint, BDPA's always talked about advancement, and how to move up to the next level. Everybody wants to move up at some point in time—well most people do—but you can't move up until you excel at what you're already doing. And in pursuit of career advancement, participating in a professional association is critically important. That's why we formed BDPA. Because in those days, you might have been the only black person in the data processing department in your company. So, it was really important for you to be able to come to a BDPA meeting and meet a Norman R. Mays, meet a Kenneth L. Wilson, meet an Earl A. Pace, Jr. The people you met at BDPA faced the same kind of challenges you did. Before BDPA, you felt alone in your organization.

Now in 2021, more of us are in IT organizations with other blacks, but guess what? You still need to have some cross-company association because maybe things aren't going well for you today where you are. Or maybe you need some new ideas to grow. So these are topics I tend to talk about in terms of how BDPA can help.

Technology Helps Everybody

Finally, if I were speaking at a BDPA Program Meeting, I would remind people that technology helps everybody—not just workers in technology jobs. I would say, "Yeah okay, you don't intend to work in an IT department, you plan to be a lawyer. That's wonderful that you're going to be an attorney. But did you know that all of your research in terms of cases will be done using information technology?" In the old days, lawyers liked to sit in the law library with all the books, but that's not how it's done now. Many of us were around when Lexis-Nexis actually started. We're old enough to remember how most of these info-tech powered tools got started. Mr. or Ms. Wannabe Attorney, these are examples of some of the technology-related proficiencies you're going to have to know in your particular job.

Teachers, parking-meter attendants, and all of us rely on technology too. Look at the technology you've relied upon during the pandemic, like Zoom, for example. Whether you're doing it from your phone, or doing it, like I am now, from my iPad, with my MAC sitting here, you're depending on technology.

Many of us, especially young people, have developed dexterity on multiple devices and platforms, regardless of what our careers or aspirations might be. So if you tell me you don't need technology, that just means you don't understand you are already using technology.

And these are the kinds of messages we need to get to the community, to black parents, to let them know that technology and automation are going to touch their lives and their kids' lives in ways they might never have imagined.

When I was Selling Software

When you're in sales, what gets you out of bed in the morning is, "What can I do to advance this deal today?" Every day when you get up, you're thinking about what can you do to progress this deal to closure. Because you have only one measurement in sales: "What have you closed lately?" In other words, what have you sold lately.

And when you're selling enterprise software, which I sold, you don't do that on one visit, or on one call; you run sales campaigns. So, thinking about how to move the campaign forward, is the kind of thing that got me out of bed during those days, which is how I achieved financial security.

In sales, when you're trying to close the deal, and the customer says no, meaning they don't want to buy, we had an adage: "The selling begins when the customer says NO." So, you learn how to handle rejection that comes with the territory of NO being thrown at you, and you learn to get up the next morning and say, "I'm going to close this deal." And those are the kinds of things you do to be successful in sales.

Building resilience during disappointments is essential in all facets of life: You're going to face challenges. You're going to face rejections. You're going to face heartbreak. However, you've got to get up and do something about it.

Getting Out Of Bed In The Morning

What gets me out of bed, and this goes to my spiritual philosophy, is, "What have I done for somebody else? Who can I help?" I have always loved doing stuff for the elderly. So, I'm always asking, "Who have I helped lately?" I like sending out cards, remembering people and calling them. I keep a "to-do" list of people I need to pray for; people I need to call, people I need to be in touch with. So, those are the kinds of things that keep me going, and every day I need to have done one of those things, or more; preferably a lot more.

Somebody once said in parallel to the "Beatitudes" in the Bible, "Blessed are those that don't remember what they have given, but never forget what they have received." So, that is a philosophy for me. People thank me for doing stuff, and I honestly don't remember. But, I can tell you what Norman Mays did for me. I can tell you what Earl Pace did for me. Those things I can tell you. But I can't tell you necessarily what I did for them. So, those kinds of ambitions wake me up, and get me out of bed in the morning.

Why We Still Need BDPA

When I walk into a BDPA meeting, I walk into a room full of people that look like me. But at the big tech conference they have in Las Vegas every year (Comdex) how many folks do you think you'll see that look like you? Still not many! Whereas, you walk into a BDPA meeting and most everyone looks like you. That's important. I was in Charlotte, North Carolina with a fellow IBM-er, and he took me to a BDPA meeting, and this was just a few years ago, and I was thrilled. It was like 1975 all over again. Unfortunately, they found out

I was a relic from the 20th Century, and they urged me to get up and give an impromptu speech about BDPA history. Yet for me, it was a thrill to walk in and see a room full of black professionals, because even now in the 21st Century, here I am selling enterprise software, managing sales teams for IBM, and I still keep going into meetings where I see nobody who is of color. So, walking into a BDPA meeting where people who look like me are facing the same kinds of challenges I'm facing, is nirvana.

I was thinking about how we can address the "Digital Divide." In America, many people don't recognize the fact that every black person doesn't live in a disadvantaged community. They talk about suburban people as if none of us live in the suburbs. And that doesn't make us better than anybody, but if we do live in the suburbs, we probably are already on the right side of the digital divide. We've got Wi-Fi in our home, we've got multiple devices, so we're blessed.

But what about the folks that don't have that? What about the black kids (or white kids for that matter) who are in homes where they don't have an internet connection, and the only way they can get an internet connection is to go sit outside a library, or a Starbucks, or tap into some other time-consuming, pride-consuming way to catch Wi-Fi? And when they miss Wi-Fi, they're more prone to miss keeping up with their classes, due to no fault of their own. Those are some of the deleterious effects of the digital divide that need to be addressed.

We shouldn't just be sitting in BDPA meetings talking about, "What do you think about the iPad Pro versus the Surface Tablet?" Those conversations are okay, and all of us who are doing well can have those kind of conversations because we've got choices. We can sit around and flatter each other, and have all those nice conversations. But what about the folks that don't have the iPhone, and don't have the cellphone capability and stuff that we do? Those of us who possess these niceties can always trade ideas and stuff about what we're doing, by virtue of already being in that kind of position.

What can BDPA do that would excite me?

Once again, it boils down to "What can we do to help those who are less fortunate than ourselves?" And, one thing we can do is act on what Norman Mays always says: "We have a moral responsibility." And ultimately, fulfilling our moral responsibility would excite me.

Like when I talked about helping seniors. I call seniors on the phone, and I've had them say, "Oh, I been meaning to send you a card. I been meaning to call." And I tell them, "Don't apologize. You've done so much for people like me all your life. It's my job to do for you now. That's my job. My job is to be calling you to see how you're feeling. My job is, if I hear you've been taken to the hospital, to show up at the ER. That's my job."

So, help somebody less fortunate than you. That would excite me.

Howard James

CHAPTER 3

Howard James

Howard James is an entrepreneur, business consultant, and IT professional. He is the Training Manager and Entrepreneurship Instructor for Women's Opportunities Resource Center in Philadelphia. Howard is Co-Owner with his wife—Dr. Karen James—of Holistic Health Suite & Café, a provider of healthy food, gourmet tea, and holistic health education and services. After earning an MBA from Eastern University, and after a 24-year IT career with the Federal Reserve Bank of Philadelphia, Howard retired as Assistant Vice President of IT in Banking Supervision. Upon retirement, he became an entrepreneur and business consultant.

Howard James is a charter member of BDPA's first chapter in Philadelphia and served as its president from 1990-92.

In a February 4, 2021, recorded interview, Howard reflected on his career, his life and BDPA.

"Never Nothing" Always do something

By Howard James

Growing up in the projects during the "gang war era" was a challenge navigating how to get out of the "tug-of-war" I was in. I had one foot in the Boy Scouts, and one foot in the gang. A lot of people didn't make it out. It was jail, drugs, or the grave. So, I was blessed to escape.

At Dobbins Technical High School, one of our teachers paid particular attention to the three young men in her mostly girl's class. She said, "Go into computers; that's going to be the thing of the future." So, we did.

We—three young men—left Dobbins and worked as Mail Boys at Food Fair Stores, and we attended computer school at night. When an opportunity came up to be a Computer Operator, we applied. A friend of ours, Steve, never applied, was never interested in computers, and had never gone to school for computers. Nonetheless, they came to the mailroom and asked Steve if he wanted the Computer Operator job. Steve was white.

So even though he was not interested, opportunity was foisted upon him. That was my first lesson in workplace discrimination, so to speak, and it taught me that we had to work harder, work smarter, and not give up. Because that was not likely to happen to us.

So, we left Food Fair Stores to get associate's degrees in data processing at Community College of Philadelphia (CCP). After CCP, two of them went into the service, and I went to work as a Computer Programmer at Pennsylvania Hospital for two years. But when I wanted to move up to a Systems Analyst, they told me I needed to work 10 years <u>or</u> get a four-year college degree. So I quit and went to Indiana University of Pennsylvania (IUP) — one of only five schools in the country in 1971 that offered a bachelor's degree in Systems Analysis.

After IUP, I became a Systems Analyst at Sun Oil Company, where I stayed four years.

Then I worked two years as a Systems Designer at CIGNA Corporation.

Overcoming Being Overlooked

When I started at CIGNA in Voorhees, New Jersey, they had, as most companies had back then, an internal computer programming training course. But when the couple of black people who came out of those programming training courses were assigned to one of the programming groups, they were given assignments as trainees, and not getting any help.

So, we would teach each other in our group, and we would teach the black trainees that weren't getting help in other groups. We would tell them, “Come over to our group. We're going to show you how to read “dumps” if they're not helping you over there.” Dumps are raw data from a computer’s memory.

One young lady came crying; she said, "They're not helping me. They expect me to know this stuff." So, we pulled her aside, "You come see us after work, for about a half hour every day, and we're going to make you better than the guy who's supposed to be training you." And we got her sharp; until she became one of the stars in that group. And she was a member of BDPA. That was an example of how being a member of BDPA helped you on your job.

The Value Of BDPA workshops

Headhunters (employment agencies) always had job offers for programmers. So in 1980, I accepted an offer at the Federal Reserve Bank of Philadelphia (The Fed).

After my first 12 years in Central IT, the President of "The Fed” wanted someone to start an IT division within the Banking Supervision area. I got the job, and moved up to an Officer, and then to an Assistant Vice President, and then was poised to be the next Chief Information Officer.

What we learned from BDPA was truly a benefit. I had a book on my desk at the Federal Reserve from when BDPA was teaching Knowledge-Based Systems and Expert Systems. When the boss came by, she said, "Why are you reading that? Do we have an expert-systems project?" I said, "No, this is a BDPA workshop, and I'm understanding this just in case there is a project." So, she said, "Oh, great. Well, then I'll know that you know this stuff if we get a project like that?"

The same thing happened when PCs first came into corporations. Through BDPA, I was studying PCs, and looking at the micro-computer Basic language, and as a result of that, when it came time for the Federal Reserve System to replace the 300-baud teletype machines that the banks were using to do funds transfers to the Fed system, I got the project, and became the project leader to head up replacing those “dumb” teletype terminals with “intelligent” PC terminals. I got to write the software that made it significantly faster than what it was with those old machines. So, any time I wanted to know something that was an emerging technology, the first place I’d go to was BDPA. We were ahead of the curve every time.

Another example was when I (along with four other BDPA members, Dave Benson, Victor Brooks, Les Holland, and Steve Peters) had our computer consulting company. One of our clients had a problem connecting a bunch of Apple Macintosh machines on the same network as some IBM PC machines, and they got this error on the network that they couldn't figure out. So, I said, "Give me that error message." I told my client, "I'll be back next week. I'm going to a BDPA conference, and I guarantee you I'll have the answer to this problem." I staked my reputation on it.

I went to conference, and this is the funny part: I'm walking through the hall with my bags to go to the hotel room, and one of the brothers from the Chicago chapter saw me and said "Hey Howard, come over here. I want you to meet one of your frat brothers from the Detroit BDPA chapter." So, I went over, we met, we talked, and I said, "What do you do, which workshops are you going to?" He said, "Well, I'm a network engineer, and I integrate different type computers on the same networks." I said, "Really?" I had this pouch on. I went in my pouch, and I pulled out this piece of paper with my question on it, "What happens when you get this error when this MAC is talking to that PC," and whatever the issue was. He said, "Oh, yeah. That's a tricky one." He said, "What you have to do is this..., then it'll work like a charm."

I called right then. I put my bags down, called my partner. I said, "Steve, go over to our client's office and try this out."

He went over there, called me back about two hours later, and said, "Like you said, it worked like a charm." And the guy who was our client, the CEO of the company, he said, "Man, I thought you were just talking trash." He said, "BDPA is pretty sharp." He said, "I want you guys to do all my computers." So, we had him as a contract for all his computers. But that was another example of using that BDPA resource to get tech projects done. It was always exciting to see the BDPA organization at work.

Teaching the Black Community

Back when we started BDPA in 1975, there were only a handful of African Americans in IT jobs. Most were keypunch operators and computer operators. Good jobs, but back then, upward career mobility started when you were a programmer. I knew three black programmers: me, Dave Benson (also a charter member), and one other person.

Earl Pace was light years ahead of all of us. He was running his own business. And Earl was more of a visionary than most of us because he was actually "there" where most of us were trying to go. So when Earl came to us with the BDPA idea, we said, "Well, that's interesting, a network of IT minded people." In the black community in 1975, I couldn't even tell anybody what I did as a job. When I told them, "I'm a computer programmer," they would ask, "What's a computer?" Keep in mind that it wasn't until 1980 that IBM released the IBM PC.

Before BDPA, blacks were not getting IT opportunities. But in BDPA, we were teaching ourselves programming techniques for practically every language that came out.

The BDPA's purpose, essentially, has not changed. From the moment we started in 1975, we said we wanted to get the African American community indoctrinated into computers, so they would at least know what they were, and what the opportunities were. We said we wanted to get more African Americans into professional jobs, and we wanted to make sure those professionals grew in those jobs. And so, that's the major thing that we have held onto for all these years.

Through our networking efforts, we connected with the Jamaican Computer Association, and when I teach in my entrepreneurship class, I emphasize the importance of starting a network as soon as you can. BDPA's original slogan, "Growth through Professional Association," sums up—in the first of those four words—the major benefit of networking. Growth!

Growing Pains

By 1978, we ran into some organizational startup challenges that almost ended BDPA. The minutes below (typed on a typewriter), from a BDPA meeting held on March 10, 1978, reflect the struggles we experienced during our early years in Philadelphia. This meeting led to what is arguably the most important decision ever made by BDPA—second only to the decision to start BDPA in the first place.

Will BDPA Survive?

OUTLINE OF SPECIAL MEETING ON MARCH 10, 1978

A special meeting was held on March 10, 1978, at the Holiday Inn, 18th and Market Street to discuss and highlight membership concerns regarding BDPA. The meeting developed as follows:

Earl Pace briefly outlined what the meeting was about indicating an informal setting and that all members were on the same level. The membership concluded the purpose of the meeting was:

What's wrong with BDPA
Should BDPA continue and how
What is BDPA's new thrust

The members decided to list their concerns on the chalkboard and develop a priority for solving the problems. Some of the concerns were:

What are the goals of BDPA
What are the purposes of the committees
What are our objectives
How can we identify our committment
Dues payment
Low attendance at workshops, lectures, and meetings
Membership mannerisms and lack of professionalism
Lack of membership committment
Profit or non-profit organization
How do we attain membership involvement

The members decided to list the critical problems on the chalkboard and vote to determine the priority for solving the problems. The problems were as follows and voting indicated the top three problem areas:

Membership interaction
Specific Goals (annual)
* Organizational Structure
Meeting Format
Resoruces Identification
* Personal committment
Professional attitude (Mannerisms)
* Specific Organizational Objectives (long-range)

*These received top priority, professional committment, specific organizational objectives, and organizational structure in that order.

The membership agreed on a vote of 14 to 4, to continue BDPA and develop a list of specific organizational objectives to be discussed at a special meeting on Friday, March 24, 1978, 6pm, Holiday Inn, 18th and Market Street.

Bottom line, we had to decide whether to continue BDPA—or not. The last paragraph in the type-written minutes above reveals our decision. "The membership agreed on a vote of 14 to 4 to continue BDPA."

Ultimately, we faced our startup challenges head on, survived and thrived.

My Time as Chapter President

I avoided being Chapter President until 1990. Earl Pace had asked me a couple of times, and other people had asked me, "Why don't you be President?" But I didn't want that responsibility because I knew how much time it would take. But here's what prompted me to run for President.

We were in Los Angeles for the 1989 BDPA National Conference. At the awards gala, every BDPA chapter had a table, or two, or three. Chicago had about five tables, but Philadelphia had zero! The founding chapter was inadvertently left off the tables list. We didn't have a table. There were five of us from the Philadelphia chapter with no place to sit, and I was not a “happy camper.”

That's when I told Priscilla Wynn Brown, who was my successor as President, that I was going to run for President. Because any time the national organization forgets to give a table to the founding chapter, that's an insult. We had become so insignificant in Philadelphia as a BDPA chapter that nobody remembered to give us a table.We eventually got a table, but I was totally upset.We had dwindled to 13 members. I told Earl, "I'm running for president," and I told him that story. I said, "When I'm finished my two years, we're going to have two hundred members."

The first year, we got 90 members. The second year, we got 100 more members. I fell short by ten, but we had 190 members by the time I left office. Back then, we didn't have any limitation on how long you could stay in office, so they tried to convince me to stay longer. But I said, "Well, I think it's better, before I get totally burned out, let's give it to one of the individuals behind me, the younger ones." My Vice President (Priscilla) ran, and she increased our chapter to over 200 members.

My philosophy was that an organization like BDPA should give people a chance to lead. That's how you build a stronger chapter. We grew under Priscilla Wynn Brown's leadership, then Victor Brooks succeeded Priscilla and lifted the chapter to a higher level, so much so that we won the National Chapter of the Year award for several years.

Our Philadelphia Chapter's rebound stemmed from our implementation of strategic planning. We called the result of that annual process, "The Philadelphia Chapter Master Plan."

We focused on marketing and collected about 100 names at the IT Career Fair. That's how the chapter grew. But the most important thing is that we prioritized building a strong chapter infrastructure (administrative policies, procedures, and retention strategies) to accommodate all of the members we planned to bring in. We became friends. We hosted card parties at each other's houses, and everybody came over, brought food, and we had picnics. We partied hard, but we worked hard, too. That friendship part made it easier to continue working together for several decades.

If you ask me what accomplishment in BDPA I'm most proud of, it's bringing the Philadelphia chapter back, because that had a significant impact on our region.

The digital divide between BDPA and the rest of the United States has narrowed considerably. It's not gone with regard to all black people, but within the BDPA family, we've narrowed the gap. You know how we have the high school computer competition teams come out in the opening ceremony with their t-shirts? Well, these young girls from Washington State, sponsored by Microsoft, they had their t-shirts on, and on the back of it, it said, "We got your digital divide." That was awesome. And they ended up winning the competition.

Before students get to the national competition, every chapter has trained them significantly in how to improve their IT and presentation skills. They know the technology. They know how to present their projects, and they get graded for every piece of that — presentation, technology, how fast the program works. And they must develop a website in about half the time as the professionals I used to hire to do it. It's amazing. They'll knock out a website in that three- or four-day period, present it, and have a working website within three or four days. We are helping our students to understand that they can be as good as they want to be.

Retirement

In spite of the fact that the Federal Reserve Bank of Philadelphia (The Fed) was looking at me as a candidate to be their next Chief Information Officer, I decided instead—after 24 years at "The Fed"—to take the early retirement so that I could become an entrepreneur and consultant fulltime.

My approach to entrepreneurship is to venture into businesses reflective of my likes and interests, then to monetize them. For example, I like martial arts, so I opened up a Martial Arts Dojo. I liked night life, so I opened a night club. My interest in computers prompted me to start a computer consulting company with four other BDPA members, as I mentioned earlier. We were doing well, but nobody would quit their day job to work the business full-time; so we closed.

My first venture into the "Tea" business started as an MBA project. At Eastern University, all MBA students had to actually write a business plan. It was called "The New Venture project." You had different professors working with you and it ran along with your MBA classes for the two years. So, when we finished, we had a tight business plan.

My MBA-class partners became my business partners. We set up an e-commerce website, and in 2000, we launched. Then, a year and a half later, we opened a storefront tearoom, and a year after that, we started building out a second location at Temple University.

But, we were running out of money. We needed $37,000 more and we didn't know where it was going to come from. We were sweating bullets.

I know prayer works because we won a $30,000 prize in two business-plan competitions. And then, a lady walked into my tearoom in East Oak Lane in Philadelphia and she ended up sending us a $10,000 check and the letter with the check said, "Because of the quality of your product and your potential for success, the business corridor is granting you $10,000." It worked out perfectly, and the moral of that story is, "Pray, never give up, and be prepared to take advantage of opportunities when they come to you."

But the bad part came in 2008. We had opened alongside six stores at Temple University in 2007, in a little mall. But when the economy crashed in 2008, the anchor store never came in, and we didn't know whether they were going to ever come in, or whether we should just cut our losses and close because we were paying $2,600/month in rent back then. So long story short, we decided in 2009 to close. We continued with the e-commerce site, and our East Oak Lane location.

After opening several cafes in Philadelphia over the years, my wife and I focused on running one, Holistic Health Suite & Café, and it's doing well. We sell healthy food, as well as smoothies and teas. We also do seminars. My wife, Dr. Karen James, is certified in classical homoeopathy, and I'm certified in specialty tea. We used to go to the World Tea Expo in Las

Vegas, every year, to get more knowledge, and that was part of our vision; to be the number one tearoom in Philadelphia. When my daughter decided that she didn't want to be the chef anymore, my wife and son decided to run the café.

Holistic Health Suite and Café

Like most businesses, we had to pivot; decide how we were going to adapt, because of Covid-19. That meant re-thinking how we were going to do business under these circumstances.

We moved to delivery and curbside pickup. And my son opened a grill in the back. We grilled salmon, chicken, and corn year round. We're doing well.

When you get a setback, think around it. I always tell a story about having to close my tearoom at Temple University. That hurt bad. It was a beautiful tearoom. But I understand what happened, and ask myself, "Could I have done anything better to make the economic crash not happen." And the answer was no. Then "How do I get past that?" You look at it as a bad situation that happened. And learn from it.

Howard James and his wife Dr. Karen James

This entrepreneurial power couple have been pillars of BDPA since the organization began. Above they are at the BDPA National Conference, in 1990, in Washington, D.C.

Life Lessons

In undergraduate school, I did not become a "serious" student until the brothers of Omega Psi Phi fraternity informed me that I had to improve my GPA to join. My grades shot up instantly, and two years ago, I was elected the Basileus (President) of the largest graduate chapter in Philly. It was a time-consuming but fulfilling undertaking.

Wow! I've been in BDPA so long, I'm trying to think back to 1975 when I was at a different point in my life, when a lot of my life was social. Out of high school, when I was that mailroom boy who wasn't even considered for that computer operator's job, what motivated me was being the most knowledgeable about computers. Another motivator was developing a more professional attitude. At a school with 10,000 students, and less than 40 Blacks, I know I had to be the best. So, I became the number one student in the Systems Analysis major, and a peer tutor/counselor.

It's about setting goals to get where you want to be and focus on achieving them. In grad school, I set a goal to get a 4.0 GPA, so I did. It was about making my mind up that I was going to master that body of knowledge in the MBA program.

At my church, I'm head of the Diaconate (Deacon Board) which keeps me involved in the church and keeps me guided by its teachings. And I'm writing an entrepreneurship book that was inspired by articles I was writing for Earl Harvey, a good friend and newspaper publisher. Earl said, "I want you to write an article called 'Howard's Small Business Tips'." I wrote tips for 18 months, then realized I had written most of the material for my book. So, I'll finish the book in the next six months, then work on other books as well.

One thing about life is — and I heard a pastor preaching about this, and it's something I heard many times before: You have to decide what people in your life are there for a season, and which ones are there for the long haul. A student of mine asked me, "What do you do about individuals who are not really in your corner, and they're kind of holding your business back." And I said, "You get rid of them; simple as that." You might love them. But if they're holding you back, don't keep trying to drag them along. Tell them you love them, but you can't roll with me on this journey. This includes friends you grew up with and even family members.

Identify those who are in your corner and those who are not and separate yourself from the latter.

If you go into business, you're a risk taker; because there is no guarantee that your business is going to be successful. You have to look at ways to mitigate the risk of failure. But you can't let something that's a setback stop you from moving forward. I didn't look at the fact that we had to close my tea café as a failure. The business knowledge I gained from that experience was priceless.

One student in my class recently said, "Is there an easier way we can do this?" I was showing them a spreadsheet that had all the variables in it to calculate the profit and loss, the cash flow statement, and the balance sheet. All they had to do was enter their numbers, and I even highlighted in yellow where to enter data. The key here is to remember that some difficult things may be the most valuable to you.

My Life Nowadays

Now that I've stepped away from the day-to-day grind of hitting urgent deadlines, I don't get up early anymore, unless I want to. I stay up late watching old cowboy movies, the Nature channel, military documentaries, or gospel videos.

But I'm always looking for something constructive to do, so I came out of retirement and began operating as a business consultant. My primary contract is with Women's Opportunities Resource Center (WORC) in downtown Philadelphia, where I serve as the Entrepreneurship Training Manager. I work about 20 hours a week, mostly helping low- to moderate-income women create business plans and start their businesses.

I also started training in martial arts again. I'm doing that to help my karate instructor to open a Dojo in Philadelphia, a karate school, where we help kids in the community. Of course, I'm not fighting in tournaments anymore, but I'm teaching the younger ones how to do what I was doing when I was fighting in tournaments. Teaching them keeps them off the streets..

I made up a slogan to help me exercise and read at least one scripture every day. Every time I get ready to not read a scripture or not exercise, I use my slogan, which is: "Never Nothing." There's never a reason to do nothing. That's what that means.

I used to always have a reason why I couldn't work out. Well now, if I'm late, I can still do 100 jumping jacks. I just say, "Never Nothing, Never Nothing, Never Nothing." And then I just start doing jumping jacks, kicks, and some punches, and if I have time, I'll do a full workout. But I will at least do something. And I'll at least read one scripture, which often leads to two or three.

If you can do something to get started, then you're often going to do more than you intended to do.

Wilbur (Mac) McReynolds

CHAPTER 4

Wilbur McReynolds

Wilbur (Mac) McReynolds, was a member of the team that developed the national organization structure of BDPA. A United States Army Veteran, Mac's business and technology career spans more than five decades. He has served BDPA in several leadership roles, including Washington, D.C. Chapter President. In a March 1, 2021 recorded interview, Mac talked about his career, his life and BDPA.

Hold On Until Reinforcements Arrive

By Wilbur McReynolds

I was born and raised in Akron, Ohio, graduated from Akron North High School, then enlisted in the U.S. Army in 1958 where I served three years as a Specialist in the U.S. Army Security Agency Europe. The Army Security Agency is the military counterpart of the National Security Agency (NSA), also known as "Big Brother."

After returning to the states, I attended Akron University part time while working at the Chrysler auto manufacturer in Twinsburg, Ohio where I worked in a production and a management trainee position.

An unexpected opportunity popped up at Diebold, Incorporated, which was world renowned as a lock and safe manufacturer. This opportunity started my Information Technology (IT) career. Leveraging its lock and safe manufacturing experience and responding to an emerging trend in the banking industry, Diebold evolved into the premier producer of automated teller machines—ATMs.

I joined Diebold's newly formed corporate internship program, and had a successful year and a half working in their Canton, Ohio world headquarters. I was then assigned as a Senior Sales Representative to the federal government in Washington, D.C. And in that role, I traveled, worked shows, did demonstrations, and stayed in Washington, D.C., for a couple of years.

Then, around 1974, I got transferred to Philadelphia where I met BDPA Founder, Earl Pace, Jr. And during several encounters, we became friends, and we've been close friends ever since.

While I was in Philadelphia, Diebold began changing their total corporate structure—worldwide. Whereas they used to have Direct Manufacturer Representatives, like me; that was my slot, so to speak. They decided to go with agencies, and they did a very nice job transitioning quickly. They cut over to the new structure on a Sunday, released me, then hired me on Monday, working as a Senior Sales Representative—and Vice President—at one of the newly formed agencies back in Washington, D.C.

The agency was like a franchise, to a degree. One of the managers that had been with Diebold is the one that was awarded the opportunity to take that "franchise" agency and continue on. For me, it was a fascinating career experience. I did a lot of things, and saw a lot of things that few have an opportunity to do. For example, I was able to access a lot of information that was confidential, secret, pretty much like it was for me in the Army Security Agency.

Joining BDPA

I met Norman Mays in the military, in Frankfurt, Germany. He popped in, and we became fast friends. When I left Germany, he was still there. He stayed in the Army. I got out.

The first time I heard of BDPA was in a conversation with Earl Pace, although I did not focus on it at that time. I thought it was interesting that he was forming this organization. But BDPA did not register in my mind as something I should be concerned with until a later conversation when Norman and I were talking, and Norm wanted to learn more about the organization that was being formed. Then me and BDPA clicked instantly, and after that, the three of us got together, hit it off, and moved BDPA's mission forward.

By 1979, our plans for building a national BDPA were coming together nicely, and the second BDPA chapter in Washington, DC was growing and flowing under the capable leadership of its chapter founder, Norman R. Mays. Then seemingly out of nowhere, Norman asked me to "hold down" the Washington, D.C. Chapter, when he was about to leave, because Norm had a once-in-a-lifetime job opportunity for himself back home in Cleveland. And to make certain I complied, Norm arranged for the other two of the "three big guys" Earl Pace and Ralph Gordon, to come help persuade me to accept their offer. It's kind of hard to go up against three big guys at one time, so I had to acquiesce, and I did accept their offer to serve as DC chapter president. But more so, it was a labor of love, because we all could see a significant growth opportunity, both locally, and nationally in cities from coast to coast. Along with my DC chapter responsibilities, my role in the national BDPA organization we had formed was serving as its first Treasurer. Driving back and forth between D.C. and Philly, we kept it all together. In May of 2009, in the photo below, the four of us had dinner together in Washington, D.C., and we reminisced about the growth and accomplishments of BDPA.

Earl Pace, Wilbur McReynolds, Ralph Gordon, Norman Mays (L to R)

As any BDPA chapter president will tell you, it's not all smooth sailing, and I faced typical organization-building challenges that ranged from having an adequate place to meet, having a significant number of attendees on a regular basis, to persuading those attendees to participate in the BDPA building process. Those challenges notwithstanding, I did manage to marshal the forces to grow the Washington, D.C. Chapter of the BDPA. And I was able to hold on until reinforcements arrived.

My technical contribution to BDPA was in the topic "Security." In my line of work, you had to be able to secure the information that you attained. You had to be able to do one of the four things that you could only do with the information at that time, and that was either to house it (storage), transmit it (electronically), transport it (physically), or secure it (keep it safe). And I was cross-trained by Diebold in all four of those areas. So, this was something that I looked forward to contributing to BDPA.

And I'm looking forward to BDPA's continued growth because the opportunities are out there, and I would really like to see BDPA go after them. For example, Congress' $1.2 trillion infrastructure package which would provide $550 billion in new federal spending over five years. What are we in BDPA doing to help ensure that an equitable portion of that spending benefits our people? We're going to have step out boldly, organize, and form coalitions with other organizations. Because if we don't, somebody else is going to get that money and we'll get left behind—again.

Meanwhile, today's D.C. chapter is one of the top chapters in BDPA in terms of the great work they're doing. We're training, certifying, and getting people jobs in IT. So we've come a long way from where we started.

My Life Nowadays

Nowadays, I 'm semi-retired, and staying involved with family and personal interests. I live in Bowie, Maryland. You've heard of Bowie State College; that's where I am. We're about fifteen miles from the White

House, five miles outside of the Beltway, which circles Virginia and Maryland. So we're in the suburbs of D.C., so to speak. Some people here don't like that terminology, "suburbs," but this is Prince George's County, the richest black county in America. It's a very cool, down-to-earth community where I live. It's cosmopolitan. It's a world center, and you can do just about anything you want to do and go anywhere you want to go from here. Life is good, and I'm hanging loose right now because I'm waiting to see what my daughter's going to do. She's very active, a licensed realtor with her own business on the side, flipping houses and so forth. I still have family in Akron. I have sisters, a brother, nephews and nieces there. So, that's pretty much "Mac" in a nutshell.

Part II

How BDPA Grew From Coast to Coast

Norman R. Mays

CHAPTER 5

Norman R. Mays

On September 11, 1982, Norman R. Mays, the new President of the National Black Data Processing Associates (BDPA), would have danced all night long, but at the precise instant the clock struck 2:00 AM, the already-ready-to-go-home custodian on duty at the BDPA National Conference Banquet hit the dance-floor lights and began pushing a 5-foot-wide "party's over" broom toward the middle of a 100-foot-long "Conga" line Norman was leading. Bopping their heads to the beat, ignoring the lights, the Conga line kept on dancing and the DJ kept on playing, until the DJ, out of the corner of his eye, noticed the broom and the collision that was about to happen.

Having grown up in the hood, the savvy-old-school DJ knew he had to act quickly. So, without missing a beat, he announced, “Last call for alcohol” while fading the funky groove into a slow song and the last dance. Satisfied that he’d made his point, the custodian turned his broom around. Pacified by the DJ’s smooth moves, the Conga line dispersed into slow-dance couples sharing smiles and conversation. The party was over. But for Norman R. Mays, life was always much, much more than a just a party.

A friendly, fun-loving socializer, the flip side of Norman Mays is that he is a hard-working, self-sacrificing, serious-minded community leader and business professional. Searching for where God wanted him to serve, he fell in love with BDPA.

During a recorded interview, transcribed below, Norman R. Mays talked about his career, his life and the growth of BDPA.

Lead, Communicate, and Grow

By Norman R. Mays

I will begin by thanking everyone who has taken the time to read what I consider to be a very interesting and important story about an organization that has made and continues to make significant contributions to the field of Information Technology (IT). As a co-author, I feel blessed to share part of my journey through life and my contributions to the success of Black Data Processing Associates (BDPA).

To set the stage, I'll start by sharing some information about myself. I grew up in Cleveland, Ohio in a neighborhood called "Glenville" in the early 1940s. In 1944, my parents bought a house on Kimberley Avenue, in the heart of Glenville (near the intersection of East 105th & St. Clair Ave). By the mid-1950s, Glenville was becoming more integrated.

My dad was a machinist (lathe operator), and my mother was a stay-at-home mom, but ran an in-home seamstress and "invisible weaving" business. Music was a major part of our household. My dad had a professional "Big Band" that performed around Northeast Ohio in the 1940s and 50s. My older sister was a classical pianist, and I was a member of a very popular R&B vocal group called *The LaSalles*. I attended Glenville Senior High School, a college-prep public school that graduated several notable persons, including former United States Senator Howard Metzenbaum, and famous actor Ron O'Neal, star of the 1972 movie *SuperFly*.

Having graduated, I was thinking about what I wanted to do with my life other than going to college. Our family could not afford college for me because the family savings had been committed to send my older sister to college at Kent State. So, I created a 3-phase plan for myself. For the first 20 years, I would work in government; for the second 20 years, I would work in the business/corporate sector; and for the third 20-

plus years, I would become an entrepreneur. To my delight, that's almost exactly how my working life unfolded.

The First 20 Years of My Career

1959 to 1979

You can't get more "government" than the United States Army where I proudly served for 20 years, from 1959 until I retired in 1979. During my first assignment in Frankfurt, Germany, I met Wilbur McReynolds, and we have been close friends ever since. We were in the Army Security Agency (ASA); the U.S. Army's European military intelligence operation.

Education

Along the path of my military career, I obtained additional education by taking courses via the military's educational correspondence program. Then I attended Fitchburg State University and Boston University while stationed in Massachusetts. Later, I attended Morgan State College in Baltimore, Maryland.

Between assignments to Vietnam, in December 1969, I graduated from the US Army Intelligence School's "Military Intelligence Officer Advanced Course" followed by a host of additional military specialty courses, including Vietnamese Language School in

Fort Bliss, TX. After Vietnam I completed training on the US Army's first IBM 360 Computer System.

Captain Norman R. Mays, U.S. Army, Stationed in Viet Nam

Vietnam

Fast forward to October 1964, and becoming commissioned as an infantry officer, I was stationed on a quiet base in the Virginia countryside. From there, in 1967, I volunteered for my first of two tours to South Vietnam. My first location was in Saigon where I served as a special assignments staff officer for the headquarters unit commander. Then, as a company commander for "A" Company, 509th Radio Research Group in Phu-Bai, where we held on through the notable Tet offensive. Phu-Bai is about 18.6 km south of Hue.

In 1970, after graduating from the Intelligence Officer Advanced Course and completing Vietnamese language school, I returned to South Vietnam for my second tour. My infantry training became extremely valuable. This time I was assigned to a small (5 US soldiers) special team where I served as an advisor to the South Vietnamese government for special intelligence operations in "IV Corps" region (the country's southernmost delta region). While there, I was awarded the U.S. Army's Bronze Star Medal and the Vietnamese government's Cross of Gallantry Medal with Bronze star; one of that country's highest military decorations. Having completed two tours of duty in South Vietnam, I was offered the opportunity to select my next assignment. I chose the field of computers and was assigned to the U.S. Army Adjutant General School in Indianapolis, IN. In June 1971 (at that school), I trained on the Army's first IBM 360 computer system where I successfully completed the specialty designation of "Automatic Data Processing Plans and Operations Officer". That began my introduction to data processing, as it was called then and is now referred to as Information Technology (IT).

Introduction to BDPA

After completing several additional intelligence related courses, I settled in at Fort Meade, Maryland and was one of the first officers assigned to the U.S. Army's newly formed Computer Systems Security unit as part of an overall military intelligence program. At that time my friend, Wilbur McReynolds, was working with Diebold Corp covering the Washington, D.C. area. He had met Earl Pace in Philadelphia and wanted me to meet him. Earl was in the early stages of forming an organization of African-Americans in the computer field and Wilbur (Mac) thought it would be great for me to get to know him. We eventually met, and I was invited to speak at one of their earliest Program Meetings. I spoke about software security and I welcomed everyone to the newly formed Philadelphia Chapter of Black Data Processing Associates (BDPA).

In 1976, I joined the "Philly" Chapter and realized that the vision of the organization was a vision that needed to be implemented across the country. We were tackling the Digital Divide long before the term became popular. In 1977, I founded the Washington, D.C.

Chapter of BDPA, and we began the national expansion. I could feel that BDPA was something new, something exciting, and something definitely needed within our community. And when I say our community, I specifically mean the African-American community. My motivation for starting the DC chapter and the national expansion came from the excitement of knowing that I could play a role in getting this critical information into our community; Information that would be needed for our future economic survival. That's what really got my energy juices flowing. I was excited about BDPA then, and I'm still excited about BDPA today. What also inspired me was I saw that there was a need for a larger vehicle for BDPA to drive in order to reach cities across the country. I shared my enthusiasm for a national organization with Wilbur McReynolds, Earl Pace, and Ralph Gordon.

Earl Pace, Wilbur McReynolds, Ralph Gordon, Norman Mays

The four of us spent hours (see my comments in "The Story Before the National Story") establishing an organization that we wanted to last for the ages, not just to satisfy a temporary whim. We've lasted more than 46 years, so we're well on our way. Though not professionally drawn, below is the original flyer for the first meeting between the Philadelphia and Washington, D.C chapter that began national conferences.

BDPA's First National Officers

When we elected our first full slate of national officers in 1980, I was elected BDPA's first National Vice President under President Earl Pace. This experience prepared me to serve knowledgeably when elected BDPA's second National President in 1981.

BDPA's First National Officers: Earl Pace, Melonese Shaw-Taylor, Myra Anderson, Wilbur McReynolds, and Norman Mays (L to R)

Four Core National Pillar Programs

Together we, the national officers, began to increase chapter membership and develop what I refer to as the four core national pillar programs that kept members excited and engaged in BDPA's mission throughout the 1980s and beyond. And steadfastly they remain core components of BDPA's program portfolio today. These four core national pillar programs that energized BDPA's rapid growth from coast-to-coast are the:

1. National Conference
2. High School Computer Competition (HSCC)
3. Chapter of the Year
4. Classroom to Boardroom

National Conference

Our *Annual National Conference* was the first (in 1979) of the four core national pillar programs that energized BDPA's rapid growth. The conference brings the best and brightest diverse talent together to discover the latest and greatest in technology and innovation. Attendees give and receive education, mentoring, business networking, scholarships and jobs.

High School Computer Competition

Launched in 1986, the High School Computer Competition (HSCC) was the first and the "flagship" Student

Information Technology Education and Scholarship (SITES) program of four current SITES programs. Today, the four current SITES programs are the:

1. High School Computer Competition (HSCC)

2. Youth Technology Camp (YTC)

3. Information Technology (IT) Showcase; and

4. The Mobile Application Showcase

Classroom to Boardroom

"Advancing Careers from Classroom to Boardroom" is a slogan that conceptualizes the essence of what BDPA is all about. First used by BDPA in the 1980s, it became a rallying cry that chapters used (and are still using) in creating and implementing community-based events. *"Advancing Careers from Classroom to Boardroom"* summarizes the wide range of career levels of the opportunity seekers BDPA helps—from classroom to boardroom. Within African American communities nationwide, we work with students from grade school through college graduate programs. And we work with tech professionals from entry level through advanced tech specialist or executive board member.

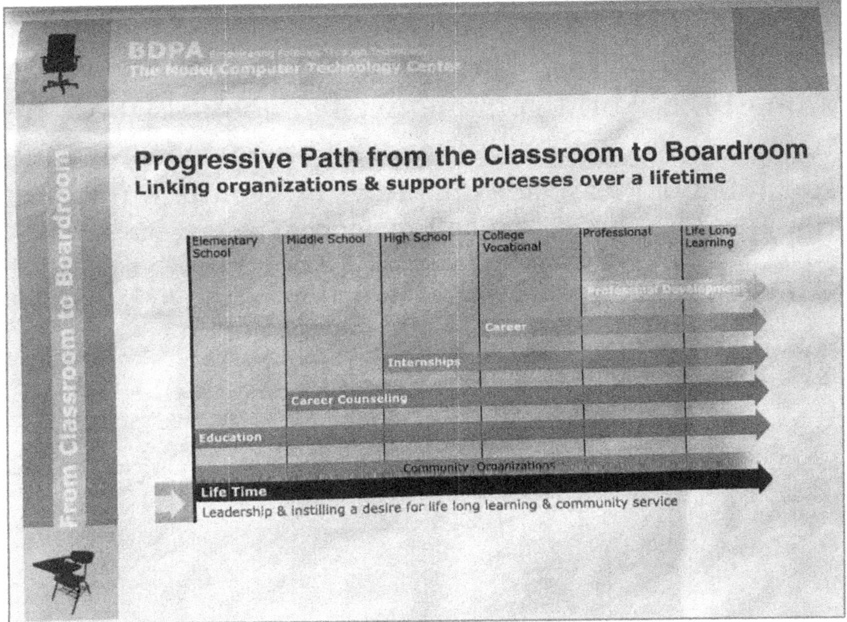

Chapter of the Year

"Chapter of the Year" is a chapter recognition program wherein each chapter submits an annual accounting of its accomplishments to a national review committee of three former national presidents. Points are awarded by category of accomplishment. The chapter receiving the most points is the winner for that year. This program has proved its worth over and over again as chapters compete to achieve excellence in pursuit of BDPA's mission.

The Information Technology Corps

In 2007, the Information Technology Corps (IT Corps)

was formed to extend the reach of BDPA beyond the borders of the USA. This opportunity to expand BDPA around the world gets me excited about BDPA's future. I often wonder how far the organization will ultimately go. Please see chapter 13 for more info about the IT Corps.

BUSINESS

BDPA Unveiled IT

May 26, 2008

Black Data Processing Associates (BDPA), an Information Technology association founded in 1975 with 50 chapters and 3,000 members in major cities in the United States, is taking a first step to establishing itself on the on the global landscape. BDPA unveiled its Information Technology (IT) Corps at the Leon H. Sullivan Economic Summit in Arusha, Tanzania at a week-long economic development conference beginning on June 2, 2008.

Norman R. Mays and Demo Solaru in Simba Hall

"This is our response to a rapidly globalizing world, and we are taking our place in it," remarked Norman R. Mays as he prepared for the trip this week. Mays, an entrepreneur and past national president of BDPA serves as the first Executive Director of the IT Corps initiative. Similar to the Peace Corps, BDPA's IT Corps will send teams of young adults on technology-based community service missions in the United States and to targeted locations abroad, particularly Africa. Mays added that "....this is an exciting new journey and we hope to engage many of the (30) African countries that have already showed interest and will be represented at the conference."

Summit primary location - Vodacom Headquarters Court Yard

In the near future, IT Corps members will assist students in African countries to review existing civic priorities and jointly devise technology based solutions that are locally effective and globally relevant. Dr. Demo Solaru, the IT Corps's Director of International Relations from BDPA's Cleveland, Ohio chapter, will participate on this trip also. An African immigrant, he maintains that "......Africa is ripe for this initiative - capacity building, knowledge sharing and transfer - our youth have the most fertile minds. In the United States, they have already showed us what's possible.... In an interconnected world, this is the logical next level...."

The premise of the Leon H. Sullivan Summit is socio- economic development in Africa through foreign direct investment. A specific area of interest to BDPA is the summit's stated objective to advance information technology through regional economic community discussions. BDPA's IT Corps student teams will be doing just that - sharing the many skills learned in BDPA's mentoring, competition and technology education initiatives in the United States with colleagues in Africa and around the world, and applying these skills to real world problems. The first student teams should deploy as early as summer 2009.

State Dinner - Venue where $5,000 equipment donation was made

info@bdpa.org
800.727.2372 / BDPA
www.bdpa.org
301.322.3474/ Office
301.322.3444/ Fax

Formed in 1996, the *Information Technology Senior Management Forum (ITSMF)* cultivates executive talent among African American technology professionals. Please see Chapter 11 of this book for more information.

BDPA National Board of Directors (NBOD)

In BDPA, we follow "Roberts Rules of Order" to establish and operate a civil organization. Roles and responsibilities are clearly defined and documented in Bylaws, Policies and Procedures at both local and national levels of the organization. New chapters applying to the NBOD to become local BDPA chapters are required to accept and abide by the national bylaws as a condition of chapter membership. NBOD members are the chapter presidents, the national officers, and two outside directors. The outside directors bring additional business-technical expertise to BDPA. Chapter presidents' NBOD participation gives them hands-on board-of-director experience in executive leadership, problem-solving and board-policy-making—all within a friendly BDPA family environment. This experience prepares them for serving on the boards of directors of other organizations, as many BDPA board members often do.

Corporate Involvement

From the beginning (for reasons of either philanthropic, community development or employee training and development) corporate support (as either in-kind services or financial donations) has been vital for the success of BDPA. Over the years, BDPA has built win-win relationships with hundreds of community-minded organizations, including Eaton, Progressive, Allstate, KeyBank, and with school systems, other non-profits, and government agencies.

For example, BDPA Cleveland Chapter, and some of our corporate backers worked together in partnership with the Anton Grdina Elementary School, under the leadership of Principal Inez B. Powell, and launched a program called the *"Student Compass Program"* that helped the school become a statewide excellent school, going from the bottom of the ranking to near the top. In the *"Student Compass Program,"* first, second, and third graders were introduced to character-building words like, truth, honesty, respect, teamwork, creativity, and dependability—exemplifying BDPA's *Classroom-to-Boardroom* concept in action. In our relationships with employing organizations, BDPA offers talented IT professionals. But we also offer outstanding corporate citizens of high moral character and integrity. At that same school, BDPA Cleveland Chapter, some of our corporate backers, and the Cleveland regional office of National Aeronautical Space Agency (NASA) worked together in a joint project, again, with the school's Principal Inez B. Powell, parents, and students to guide students in building a replica of NASA's space shuttle along with individual student experiments. These student science projects advanced the viability of offering STEM education to first, second, and third graders in inner-city school systems. The overwhelming success of the project was touted in a worldwide NASA publication. And accompanying that publicity, the late

Congressman Louis Stokes attended a reception celebrating that achievement.

Principal, Inez B. Powell, NASA Director, Daniel Goldin, Congressman, Louis Stokes (Left to Center)

NASA Astronaut Charles F. Bolden, Jr., Norman R. Mays (Seated in Front)

The Second 20 Years of My Career

1980 to 2000

The first 20 years of my career flew by faster than a military fighter jet. I served my country honorably and retired from the Army with the rank of Major. Prior to my retirement, I was introduced to a life-changing organization called BDPA. Then moving back to my hometown Cleveland, Ohio, I began the second 20 years of my career working for Eaton Corporation. Soon thereafter, I reconnected with old acquaintances, met new friends, and founded the third chapter of BDPA in 1980.

Working for Eaton, I had to adjust to working in a data processing department in a corporate environment verses the military environment that I had grown to love. However, I had prepared for the transition, and the change helped me grow personally and professionally. As the Manager of Data Security and Contingency Planning for the Eaton Corporation, the challenges were always present. Prior to the recession of 1981-82, I overcame those challenges. It was a productive and satisfying stay at Eaton. But Eaton, like most companies, was hit hard by that recession, and downsizing had become an all-to-common event.

I was not spared, and after several months seeking new opportunities, I went to work for Cole National Corporation in the same capacity—again, productively and satisfyingly—until the next recession, which arrived way too soon. That's when I decided to leave the corporate environment and move on to my third 20-year phase of my career.

The Third 20 Years of My Career
2001 to Present

Having participated in the entrepreneurial process of growing a national BDPA organization, and founding and growing two BDPA chapters, my small business development skills were sharp. Those BDPA experiences coupled with the fact that I've always been a person who enjoys engaging with people of all backgrounds led me to pursue several major entrepreneurial ventures.

One venture was with *Network 2000*, a company that represented *US Sprint* (Now *Sprint*) during the roll out of their high-tech fiber optic long distance service. I did well. The other major venture is in the field of financial services. I'm still doing that today.

In both ventures I was exposed to many modern technologies—always a major plus for me. Equally important were the opportunities I had to utilize leadership skills I acquired as a commissioned Army officer, in various corporate situations, and in BDPA. Utilizing these business-building skills has been productive and gratifying. And over the years, BDPA has provided numerous opportunities to teach what I've learned to others. There are few things in life more satisfying than seeing someone you mentored, succeed and grow.

A volunteer organization, BDPA members are sometimes pressed into leadership roles with no prior training or experience. But that's one of the great things about BDPA, and that's one of the main moments when BDPA's original slogan "Growth Through Professional Association," goes into action. In BDPA, we teach technology, and we teach leadership. And we do this teaching in a "BDPA Family" environment where we push members toward excellence but we always cushion their occasional fall with encouragement, with the know-how of other members, and with hand-holding if needed. BDPA is a proving ground for leaders in business and technology, and over the ages, leadership development has always been a key to building successful organizations.

Throughout all of my entrepreneurial pursuits, I have stayed connected with BDPA and technology, and will always continue doing so. From BDPA, I have learned that the only limits on what we can achieve are those we place on ourselves.

When Earl Pace, Wilbur McReynolds, Ralph Gordon and I brainstormed BDPA's future, we had no idea BDPA would become so splendid. It makes me feel like a "Proud Papa" when I see BDPA's success.

Dr. Jesse Bemley

CHAPTER 6

Dr. Jesse Bemley

The founders of Historically Black Colleges and Universities (HBCUs) overcame formidable odds and answered their call to serve with heroic passion and purpose. They formed *circles of success* between students, teachers, and financial backers to do what seemed impossible.

An 1831 Virginia law forbid the education of slaves, free blacks, and mulattos. But that changed following the Civil War, and Hampton Institute was founded soon thereafter, in 1868.

Born a slave and graduated from Hampton Institute, Booker T. Washington, at only 25 years old, co-founded Tuskegee University in 1881. In the formative years of Tuskegee, students provided the labor for constructing school buildings and working the school's farm lands.

In his autobiography, *"Up from Slavery"*, Booker T. Washington wrote, "We began with farming because we wanted something to eat." In those formative years, to survive, grow their education, and grow the university, students worked all day farming and constructing, and attended to their academic learning during classes in the evening.

This unrelenting, entrepreneurial circle of success exemplifies a relentless commitment to the cause of educating freed slaves. In order to survive in those turbulent times, freed slaves worked hard, trusted, and depended on each other and their benefactors.

Bent but never broken, that same work ethic has persisted and remains in our veins. And today, more and more employers are discovering what has always been true: When paid equitably, the employment of black American workers is America's best bang for its labor-purchasing buck.

◆

Born in Memphis, Tennessee and graduated from Mississippi Valley State University, Dr. Jesse Bemley pushes his students toward excellence as if their lives depend on it, because—as Dr. Bemley knows from real life experiences—they do.

More than a motivator, Jesse is the Founder of the Joint Educational Facilities organization, an all-volunteer, non-profit, community-based organization that helps junior and senior high school students learn advanced computing science, mathematics, and intelligent technologies. Dr. Bemley earned a Master's degree from American University, and a Ph.D. from Pacific University.

Jesse is also the founder of the BDPA High School Computer Competition and the IT Showcase—two award-winning programs that have revolutionized the entire BDPA organization.

In a May 27, 2021 recorded interview, Jesse talked about his career, his life and BDPA.

Push Students Toward Excellence

By Dr. Jesse Bemley

I was born in Memphis, Tennessee in 1944, the oldest of five children. We were a welfare family and didn't have much back in those days. Growing up, I was anxious to get to Hamilton High School where I did exceptionally well. My best friend (Melvin) and I excelled in math and were always competing against each other; friendly competitiveness. Melvin had a brother who went to Morehouse College right after the end of his 10th grade year in high school, and that got us thinking about going to college.

Mississippi Valley State Band

I was away from my high school, the day that Mr. Russell Boone from Mississippi Valley State brought his band to Memphis to give concerts at each of the seven black high schools in the city at that time. The reason that he brought his band up was to do some recruiting. He would give a concert at each of the schools, then after his concert, he would have auditions. But when he came to my school, I was at LeMoyne College at a math contest representing my high school. I didn't win, of course, but it was an all-day event, and at the end of the day, I returned to my high school for band practice. We had a good practice that day, I remember it very distinctly.

After practice, our band director, Mr. Doggett, said, “Bemley, you know that Valley State came in and gave a great concert this morning.” And he said, “I know you were at the college in the math contest, but Mr. Boone's looking for baritone horn players, and I told him that I had one of the best baritone horn players in the city.” Well, he kind of exaggerated that a bit, but he says, “Mr. Boone left this for you.” And it was a scholarship; it was a scholarship to Mississippi Valley State, but it wasn't a full scholarship. Because with this scholarship, you needed another $300 to go with it.

I always carried my baritone horn home with me, and it was about two miles from the school to home. And even though I was the smallest kid in my class, walking through a rough neighborhood, carrying a baritone horn, I made it home safely with no conflicts that day. And when I got home, man, I was so excited, I told my Momma, and Momma says, "Well, you know, we talked about this, and you still need money to go with this, and you know we don't have that." So, that burst my bubble.

As luck would have it, my high school English teacher found a job for me, then convinced her professional organization of black teachers that the annual $300 scholarship they gave to one student at my high school should go to me. So now, all I needed was a ride down to the Mississippi Valley State campus. And fortunately, one of my classmates who got a scholarship there too, says "My family's gonna drive me down there, and I'll ask my dad if you could ride with us." And the next day, he said, "My dad says, 'Hell yeah' you can ride with us."

We arrived at Mississippi Valley State

I majored in math because Mississippi Valley State was so small it didn't have majors in my first two choices; Electronic Engineering and Physics. And I'm happy it happened that way, but a lot of people thought that I was a "Music" major because I was in the band. My roommate and I started a free tutoring service helping other students on campus. And I graduated with a BS degree in Mathematics, in three years; number five out of a class of three hundred. In the process, I made the Dean's List in every quarter—except one.

But after graduating, I was so poor, I didn't have enough money to get home with my degree. And so, I had to get money from the Dorm Director, and he says, "Bemley, I want to buy you this bus ticket, and I want to see you doing some great things."

Back Home in Memphis

So I got home to Memphis. And that three years of college was probably the best thing that ever happened to me because it was the first time I had ever been any further than 80 miles away from home. I went to Indianapolis twice; played in "Indianapolis 500" parade; got a chance to sit in the grandstands there. We were the first all-black band to play in the "Tournament of Roses Parade" out there in Pasadena, California. And we were all over the South because the band went everywhere the football team went. So I was well traveled by the time I graduated.

However, there were no jobs back home, and I didn't want to be a teacher. So I am thankful that while I was at Valley State, my adviser would not let me register for my classes unless I registered for some Education courses. And I told him, "Why do I want to do that? I want to be a Mathematician; I don't want to be a teacher." He said, "Well okay, that's really good. But I'm not going to sign off on your registration form until I see some Education courses." And he knew what he was doing because he said, "Suppose there's nothing else available to you." And sure enough, I was back home with my degree in Mathematics, but there were no jobs for me, and I got to the point where I went to interview for a Bank Teller job, but I didn't get hired for that either.

Teaching Math

I got a call from a gentleman at Moss Point, Mississippi, on the Gulf Coast, at Central High School, and he asked me if I was teaching, and I told him no, because I was all set to go to the Air Force; this was in November, and in December, I was all set to go to the Air Force. I had determined that, "Maybe I'll just go on to the military." He says, "You want to work for me?" I said, "What would I be doing?" He said, "Teaching math, what you've been trained for." I told him, "Well, I would, but I can't even afford to get all the way down from Memphis to Moss Point, and even if I get down there, I wouldn't have anywhere to stay." He says, "If you get down here, I'll take care of the rest." And I stayed down there for a year, and taught high school mathematics—and I kind of liked it.

I worked as a Cartographer.

Well, at the end of the school year, I went home, of course, and I got some information about a job as a

Cartographer at the United States Air Force's "Chart and Information Center," in St. Louis. I did some real simple math: At the high school, I made $3,600 per year teaching, and these people were going to offer me $6,451 per year. Back in 1965, six thousand dollars was a lot of money. So, I went to St. Louis on a bus from Memphis and started my new job.

U.S. Military

Three months later, I got my greetings letter from the President of the United States. This was in 1966 during the Vietnam War. And so, I had to go back home to be inducted into the Army. When I was inducted, they put us on a bus, took us downtown to the train station, where we boarded a train to Hopkinsville, Kentucky.

After twelve weeks, they sent me to Fort McNair in downtown D.C. It was great. We had our own vehicle. I mean, it was the vehicle that the group of us used to get back and forth between Fort McNair and Army Map Service, which is where we worked. We were working as Mappers.

After the Army

In September 1968, after being honorably discharged, the Army Map Service decided to hire me as a Mathematician; although it really was a glorified Fortran Programmer job. One of the guys at Army Map

Service, who was a Cartographer, became the Executive Director of the D.C. Board of Elections. The D.C. Board of Elections had a one-person data-processing department, and that one person was borrowed from the Statistics Office of the D.C. Government.

So when the Cartographer took over down there, he needed to get his own person. Long story short, I became that person. And over time, I made the transition from the FORTRAN to the COBOL language; equally challenging was the fact that I worked with UNIVAC and Honeywell equipment, and I was walking into a shop that used IBM 360 equipment. But I overcame those challenges, and everything ended up okay. Once I got the hang of it, I became a legend at the D.C. Board of Elections.

Drug Enforcement Administration

With that mission accomplished, I knew it was time to start looking elsewhere for my next challenge.So, I walked five blocks to the Drug Enforcement Administration (DEA) because their Narcotics and Dangerous Drug Information System (NADDIS), that was written in IBM Assembly language, needed to be updated and written in COBOL.

They were moving to COBOL because—for the DEA and for organizations across America—writing programs in Assembly languages had become difficult when compared with the relative ease and speed of writing programs in COBOL. So programmers weren't bothering to learn Assembly languages anymore. Long story short, the DEA needed COBOL people and I got a job with them. So, I was writing programs in COBOL for the DEA, and enhancing some other programs that were already written in COBOL. And while I was doing that, they needed me to enhance another system, and introduce COBOL modules into it. Systems had to be no larger than 4 Kilobytes (4K). Now being one of those early programmers from back in the days when, if your program was one byte too big, that was it; that was the end of your program. So, I wrote the first COBOL/CICS module; that was on the DEA CICS system. At first, I could not get it any smaller than 8K. So I created two 4K modules, and those modules are still in use. And they made a decision that they would not do this big COBOL overhaul that they had envisioned, because the consequence and cost for the relative ease and speed of writing programs in COBOL, is that those resulting COBOL modules use up way more Kilobytes of memory workspace than do Assembly programs. So, I wrote Assembly modules when COBOL modules were too big and inefficient to fit. And that's what I did for them: I wrote CICS using Assembly language. And I stayed on, and continued supporting those systems.

Strayer College

During that period of time, I was a military veteran . I said to myself, "You know, maybe what I can do is take a couple of classes at Strayer College, using 'GI Bill' money." And I did that, and I got to know the Computer Science Department Chairperson very well, and he talked me into becoming the Strayer College Assembly Language Teacher for the next six years. I got to be Assistant Chair, and taught the three classes that the seniors took: Management of a DP Organization; Management Information Systems; and a Data Systems Seminar.

While I was teaching for him, the Chair had just finished getting his Master's degree at American University, and suggested, "Jess, why don't you go down and get your Masters? You could do this." I said, "Well, how am I going to teach?" He said, "Aw, you'll be able to do it." And I got my Master's degree from American University while I was teaching at Strayer, and while I was working full time for the Drug Enforcement Administration.

How I Heard about BDPA

It was in 1983, I was an avid reader of "Computer World" back in those days, and I saw the article about a BDPA Conference at the Hilton Gateway Plaza Hotel in Newark, New Jersey. So I called the hotel, left my information, and within an hour, I got a call. I can't remember the man's name, but he was telling me, "Oh yeah, we've got a DC chapter, and Shirley Ginwright is the President. He gave me Shirley Ginwright's phone number. I called Shirley, and we chatted a short time, and not long after that was when the conference actually happened, and so that's when I met her in person at the Newark conference. And you're talking about a happy guy. My wife and I rode up to Newark on the train, and we got off the train right there at the hotel. And everybody I met, I kept telling them how excited I was that I was there, and that I wanted to become a part of what was going on. I was a member of the Association of Computer Machinery (ACM), but the thought of an organization for Black DP professionals was an idea that I wanted to be a part of. And I tried to show BDPA membership some of the things ACM was doing that BDPA was not doing, and fittingly, the 1983 Conference theme was, "Rise to the Challenge."

□

Expert Systems

I introduced "Expert Systems" to BDPA. We had a lot of entrepreneurs in BDPA during that time. And I was trying to let them know that, hey, here, you could get an expert system shell for one hundred bucks, and you could take one of your data entry people and let them play around with this for maybe one hour a day, to develop a learning curve, because it was a lot of money going around during that time, in expert systems. But the idea didn't catch on in BDPA, so I launched it at my non-profit organization, the Joint Educational Facilities (JEF), and one of my college students decided we were going to teach expert systems to high school students. And so in 1987, in New Orleans, the year after the High School Computer Competition (HSCC) started, I introduced, along with three high school students, the JEF Artificial Intelligence (AI) Model of a Black Teenager.

The Conference, IT Showcase, and World Congress on Expert Systems

At the 1987 BDPA conference, I flew into New Orleans, took a shuttle to the hotel—that must have been around Tuesday—and I did not leave the hotel until Sunday morning on my way to the airport. That's because I was responsible for all HSCC activities, security and everything, and IBM had loaned BDPA the equipment. But I was happy when I left because it was a success.

As mentioned in the introduction, the Joint Educational Facilities (JEF) is an all-volunteer, non-profit, community-based organization that helps junior and senior high school students learn advanced computing science, mathematics, and intelligent technologies.

By design, the IT Showcase that members see at BDPA Conferences was based on the JEF model that we launched at JEF in 1982. Starting with New Orleans, in 1987, I was taking kids to the conference with me. And in my presentations, I would have them make their mini-presentations, because I'm always trying to make things better and give the young people more of a platform, and more of an audience. And so I got to the point where, I wanted them to have their names on the program. And Midge Johnson, and Vivian Wilson came to me and said, "Jesse, you need to bring your students to the BDPA Conferences every year." So I did, and in the year we started that, at the 1995 Conference in Kansas City, my kids presented their own "Showcase" program within the BDPA Conference. So, that's the basis of the IT Showcase.

What we would make the students do is; we would give a student a project, and the student would work this project, but as they worked this project, they took notes. And during the project, the first thing that they had to do is, they had to become subject-matter experts in that area, and that would be the first paper they had to write; it would be a minimum 10-page paper. Then, once they had mastered the subject matter, they would actually start working on a project within that subject area. And they would document that, and at the end of the project, the student has two papers; one which shows their knowledge of the subject matter; and the other one is documenting the project that they had done.

When we were at the 4th World Congress on Expert Systems (4thWCES) in 1996 in Mexico City, there was a gentleman who heard my JEF students speak. And he said, "Your high school students are doing the same thing that I had to do for a master's thesis at the university in Colorado."

But what I'm trying to do is to get more of our students talking and presenting because I want more of them getting advanced degrees. And what we're doing now is we're fixing it so that these kids can make money without having to get advanced degrees, because that's what the Biden administration is doing. I keep telling my young people; if you can't play on the world stage, then you're going to get "clocked," or get your "bell rung." Because these other people, they're not dumbing their stuff down, and we're not dumbing our stuff down either.

BDPA needs people working in the trenches

I was asked, "Jesse, why don't you run for National President?" "No, no, no, I don't need that," was my answer to that question whenever I was asked. And I've never regretted not being one of the national officers, and the rationale is this: I was so happy to be a part of the BDPA, and I saw so many things that could be, and should be done. And to do those things, BDPA needed more people in the trenches. And to me, that's where the action was, and that's where I wanted to be, to help build the organization. And so, that's where I have been the whole time.

The year after Newark was the Cleveland Conference. And the DC crew all piled into Shirley Ginwright's van, and we rode up to Cleveland together, and that's when we got the name "The Rabble Rousers."

At the Cleveland Conference, Gerard Anderson became the National President, and Gerard says, "Jess, you've got to do something, man. Why don't you be National Education Committee Chair?" Gerard wanted me to start, and be the Chair of a National Education Committee, but that didn't happen right away, because every time I thought of something, people were scared of it. For instance, the High School Computer Competition; for instance doing our national conferences on HBCU campuses. People were scared of it, or let me put it this way; people were afraid of doing something different. The reason new ideas were being shot down is because people hadn't been exposed to the new ideas I was proposing. That was the problem. And I guess, if I had run for President, we could have done some of those things, but I don't regret not having been President. I just get so much joy out of seeing students at the conference.

But I did eventually accept Gerard's offer, and I became National Education Committee Chair. And so, what I came up with, at the time that Gerard asked me to be Education Committee Chair, is: We only had two college chapters in BDPA; one in Cleveland at Cleveland State, and the other one in Philadelphia, at Temple University There was no high school presence at our conferences. You've got to have some kind of pipeline, in order to keep feeding young talent, so that the organization doesn't just die out. And so I came up with this High School Computer Competition (HSCC) because our sports arenas are always full, and there's a lot of money out there in that. But, we were not really pushing our academic prowess. And the HSCC was something that included chapters and that could be embraced by the national organization.

Washington, D.C. Team Wins BDPA Computer Competition

The initial pilot HSCC competition took place at our 1986 Conference in Atlanta. During the competition, I saw those young people square off across the room; and this was in the big computer lab at South Side Comprehensive High School, now the Maynard Jackson High School, that was a magnet school for computer science at the time. When those kids started collaborating with each other on their teams making decisions about the various tasks, I knew I had done the right thing. The pilot was a huge success, and at the next National BDPA Board meeting, the High School Computer Competition (HSCC) was voted a BDPA National Initiative.

Since then, the HSCC has grown from the two pilot teams to at least 15-20 teams per year ever since. And over the years, the competition has blossomed from a "question-and-answer session" and a "BASIC programming application" competition, to a "web application development" and "team presentation" competition.

My Life Today

Nowadays, what gets me up in the morning, is my wife. She's got to be at work at seven o'clock, and so I get up and take her to work. When I retired from the federal government, back in 2010, I told her I did not like her riding the subways or busses, so I was going to take her to work every day, and I've been doing that.

Then, it must have been about four years after retirement, I told her, "You know, I've got to teach a college class, or something, before I lose my vocabulary." And that was about the time that the Bowie State University opportunity came along, so I taught there part time for a while. I am now a fulltime lecturer.

Where should BDPA go from here?

In advising where BDPA should go from here, I like what this current BDPA administration is doing; the technology they're using to get things done.

The thing that hasn't been done, that I would have liked to have seen, was for us to have a more robust regional activity structure. The best initiatives are launched from the bottom up; not from the top down.

And as these young people mature and come up and out, we've got to figure out how far and fast to push them, because, they've got lives too. And everybody isn't going to take half their life to do the type of work that we think they should do.

It's like my son—he is Chief Information Officer (CIO) of the JEF organization. And he's got a lot of great ideas, but he just doesn't have the time to implement them. He's in this cyber-security subject area, like that last big bug that hit the federal government and the petroleum industry. He is so tied up working on cyber security, that he can't do, on a voluntary basis, all that he would like to do for JEF. So with my son and others, I'm still out here fighting that battle, trying to help people help themselves.

Build relationships as you learn

What I tell students is this: When you walk into a class, you have to learn the subject matter because that's for you. You're going to need that subject matter when you get out there in the world in terms of your career endeavors. But you also need to think in terms of learning your instructor. If you learn your instructor, what you wind up doing is, learning how to anticipate what that person is going to ask you, what type of scenarios that person is going to give you, thinking like that person, and if you do, and if that person is a person that is subjective, you're going to always get an "A" in that class.

Nowadays, that's more and more difficult to do because a lot of our education is being automated online. And I like that in one way, but in another way I hate it. I hate it because I don't really get a chance to know my students. A student might say, "Dr. Bemley, I was in your Linux class, and I got an "A" out of the class. Can I get a letter of recommendation from you? But the problem is, I don't know him or her. If I'm going to write a letter of recommendation for you, and if you're really serious about me doing it, the least you could do is send me your resume along with the request. And don't just say that you are trying to find a job; let me know who you are, where this letter is going, to what organization, these kinds of things. That's what I'm telling my young people. I have office hours, even though they're remote. You could come in (remotely), and you would learn a little bit about me, and I could learn a little bit about you, and I could know what kind of circumstances you are living with, that kind of thing. Because, I've been a student once, and I'm only too happy to help if I can. But if you don't come to me, then I won't know. And I try to get students to come to BDPA activities because they need to start developing their network.

So, even though you're learning through technology, you still have to form relationships with people through the technology.

We still need BDPA

It's 2021, we still need BDPA, and I'm still here and so I can at least make myself available to young people who might want to talk to me. Because at the end of the day, I am a teacher, and from my perspective, organizations like BDPA exist to be platforms upon which my students can build and develop themselves. And the primary reason I work so hard for BDPA is so that I can have a little bit of "say so" in terms of where my students can present the results of their research, which helps in their development. And I'm proud that the students even want to talk to me. Because, I'm one of those welfare kids that grew up, and when they think that I have something to say that they can latch on to, I'm only too happy to say it, because (and I've been saying this all the time) our country could have been so much further ahead than where it is now, had the country just respected and developed our community.

Meanwhile, in BDPA, we've got to keep on respecting ourselves and developing ourselves with everything we've got.

Vivian Clara Wilson

CHAPTER 7

Vivian C. Wilson

Energize Your Organization's Culture

Organizational culture is built on faith of values and beliefs, and is more foundational to an organization's success than strategy could ever be. Great leaders like Vivian C. Wilson knew this, and taught us that unfolding family feelings of warmth and worth, while unleashing perpetual power enough to change the world begins with a simple hug—The BDPA Hug. Vivian's tough love ran telephone billing for the entire state of Ohio, and her decision to share that wisdom with BDPA came right on time when she was, in 1989, elected the first female President of National BDPA. We already had an amazing mission when she arrived, but we needed to be brought back together as one family—which she immediately did.

At the Ohio Bell Telephone Company, Vivian worked her way up the corporate ladder. And after 33 years of service to Ohio Bell, and the subsequently formed Ameritech Corporation, Vivian retired as Data Center Manager. Twenty of those years of service were in Computer Operations, Security, and Data Systems.

In 1992 Vivian formed a Partnership with Ohio Bell and John Adams, and in doing so, gave back to her beloved high school by making positive improvements in the neighborhood. For this outstanding effort, she was recognized by the school, neighborhood, and city. Vivian exemplified what it meant to be a John Adams Rebel for life.

For BDPA, Vivian received the very first "Board of Directors National Outstanding Member of the Year". She was elected National Vice-President in 1987, and elected National President in 1989. Ms. Wilson served as National BDPA's President from 1989 to 1992, and was selected in 1990 as Cleveland's Professional Woman of the Year.

The greatest increase in BDPA Chapters occurred under Vivian's presidency, and some of BDPA's greatest and most memorable national conferences occurred when, after her two terms as President, Vivian formed a national conference team that professionalized how BDPA conducted its Annual National Conferences.

Vivian joined Karamu House Theater in April 1998. She enjoyed the energetic atmosphere of Karamu House while working with people of all ages from toddlers in the daycare, youth involved in various groups, to adults and seniors. She relished interfacing with people from all walks of life, in various volunteer activities, tours and classes that were offered at Karamu. Vivian never met a stranger, and welcomed you with a smile and/or a hug. It was often said and written that Vivian was the "face of Karamu House to the world." During her tenure there, Vivian served as Marketing Manager, Interim Cultural Arts & Education Coordinator, Interim Early Childhood Development Director, Director of Resource Development, and Sales & Marketing Director. Vivian retired from Karamu House Theater in May of 2014.

The Interview Visit

On January 14, 2020, Norman Mays, and I (Ken Wilson) visited Vivian at her home to interview her for this book. The visit was a get-back-in-touch social visit as much as an interview, and we actually recorded only a few of her words with the intent of conducting a more formalized interview later. Her daughter Marie Tracey was there too, so it seemed like old times again. Tragically, we would never see Vivian again, as she passed away on October 19, 2020.

Even so, her legacy of love lives on. And respectfully, a few of these fond memories of her are shared below.

Vivian Lifted the Entire BDPA Organization

It was in October of 1985, when after a BDPA Program Meeting, I (Ken Wilson) had given Vivian a lift home, per her request, and we were talking about BDPA, as we tended to do after those monthly family reunions we call Program Meetings. We were sitting in her driveway with the engine of my 1984 Oldsmobile 98 Regency idling. The ride was so smooth, it felt like the car was turned off. We were both "Wilsons," but we had never traced any blood or marriage lineage between us. Nonetheless, we both knew that she was always my big sister, and I was always her little brother. Cleveland Chapter elections were next month, and as we sat there, engine purring, I suggested, "You would be a great President. I'll be your Vice President." But she said, "No, you be President, and I'll be your Vice President." And that's what we did, and behind that impetus, and behind the impetus of great people in our chapter like Vivian, Norman, George Williams, Barbara Whitfield, Henry Ford, Bill Darling, Gerry McClamy, Hank Lawson, Cassandra Suttles, and more, Cleveland won several Chapter of the Year awards. And we are proud to have carried the original torch that ignited the Chicago fire, that ignited fires in BDPA chapters from coast to coast, causing members to murmur, "If Cleveland can do it, I know we can do it." And those accomplishments and accolades all occurred because of the admiration we, BDPA members from coast to coast, feel for each other, and the love we feel for BDPA. And all of that love was deepened and enriched by Vivian's "BDPA Hug." Because when we hugged, tensions among members melted immediately. And we laughed, were more comfortable, and were more competent in carrying out our working assignments. We got a lot more work done.

And Norman and I did, on that last visit with Vivian, capture a few of her final affections for BDPA, and those words she shared, that were also played at her memorial, in her original voice, are transcribed below.

In Her Own Words

By Vivian C. Wilson

Recorded January 14, 2020

What I found in BDPA was a wide range of friendships. I'm talking Earl Pace. Look at all that he has accomplished. And then there was Norman who I enjoyed picking on tremendously. And you just need someone who will let you spill out all the things that are blocking you that would give you an answer or a solution: "Well, have you tried this, have you not tried that?" And I saw that approach starting to help all of the folk in BDPA, whether they were in management, or not. But you had to listen. That was free information that came to you from all kinds of ways. It was good times. Now, we had good times after we got all our work out the way.

I met and had a discussion about this with my best friend in the world, Margaret (Midge) Johnson, who was interacting with a group of folks out of Washington, DC. And she just threw my brain out of whack, when she said such an organization existed. Didn't realize I was going to be running around the country. But each time we met a person, or knew of a person that was really sticking to it, and doing something in the field, Midge went after them one way, and I went after them another way. And we were—I was totally amazed at how many people were of the same mindset. We looked out for each other, and it was an absolutely fun time. But that's what a professional organization should be; a place where you have something in common that's big enough to keep your mind occupied.

George Williams

CHAPTER 8

George Williams

George Williams is a long-time member of BDPA Cleveland who has served BDPA in several leadership roles including Cleveland Chapter President and National President from 1994 through 1999. George was a leader on the team that introduced the Enterprise Transformation Process (ETP) to BDPA, a process that enhanced how BDPA operates. Following a 30-year Information Technology career working within corporate, civic, and non-profit environments, George now shares these experiences as an independent business coach, counselor and business advisor. In a July 14, 2021 interview, George talked about his career, his life and BDPA.

Listen. Build Consensus. Move Forward

By George Williams

I am a Clevelander, born at Lakeside Hospital in 1954 and raised here. My parents are from Mississippi who came to Cleveland in the early 50's to start their family in the Glenville area. For the first fourteen years of my life, my destiny was to be a Glenville High School Tarblooder.

One day on a Friday, my parents came home and said, 'we're moving.' And the next thing I knew, I was going to be a John Adams High School Rebel. We moved in 1969 when I was 14 years old. There had been a lot of civil unrest in the summer of 1968 after the Reverend Dr. Martin Luther King was assassinated. Growing up in Glenville, I saw the National Guard sitting on their jeeps with machine guns waiting for something to happen.

I cried like a baby when they moved my three siblings and I, but it is probably the best thing they could have done for us, to move out of Glenville, which was starting to turn in a different direction. I have an older brother, Wallace, and two younger sisters, Denise and Debra, who are now all in Atlanta along with my mom. They continue to entice me to move down there but that's another story.

John Adams was a great time. I joined the JV football team, moved up to varsity in my junior and senior years. I was recognized as somewhat of an elite

Middle Linebacker that received some college offers. But I had to take a hard look at myself and figured out I was too short and too slow which brought that career path to an end.

I had already recognized that college prep studies were not for me. I knew that I was not a studier and liked to go down to Kent State, meet my cousins and party. College did not appear to be the right path for me so I went to my guidance counselor and asked, "What else you got?" She said, "Auto Shop, Woodshop, Home Economics, and Accounting and Computing." So I'm like, "What's Accounting and Computing?" It was an Introduction to Computers of the early 1970s, which were Card Sorters and 5081 punch cards. So Accounting and Computing became my path for the next two years at John Adams where I studied Bookkeeping and the basics of Data Processing – which has been with me to this day. One of my biggest accomplishments was to learn how to type and at my best, I hit 90 words a minute with no errors. I carry that to this day, not 90 words a minute, but the ability to translate and document my thoughts and subjects quickly. I give all the credit to John Adams and Miss Johnson the Vocational Education Instructor and typing teacher.

Launching My IT Career

In 1972 one month out of high school I got a call from the Ohio Bell Telephone Company who had adopted the Vocational Program at John Adams. The next thing I know, I'm driving from the Mount Pleasant area to Brecksville Ohio to work as a third shift Computer Operator. It was like driving from Earth to the Moon. There were significant differences between the neighborhoods, but more particularly, for the first time I was in a company where I was the only black guy on my shift.

I learned later, that former National BDPA President, Vivian Wilson, who was also a John Adams alumnus, was part of the team that had adopted the school. Although I didn't know about it at the time, it was through her efforts that I got into Ohio Bell that started my DP career path. She was there as a Job-Control Scheduler, and 15 years later, we met again in BDPA and became great friends, however meeting Vivian when I was 18 is a great memory.

I left Ohio Bell to go to the City of Cleveland as a 2nd shirt Computer Operator where I met future BDPA member Gerry McClamy. I left the City to work at Glidden-Durkee, a Fortune 500 company as a Computer Operator.

After 4 years, I left to work for a small company on the West Side of Cleveland called C-Trac, where once again, I was the only black guy working for this Computer Service Bureau. It was an opportunity for me to learn about small business since this was truly a startup situation where you wore a lot of different hats.

After starting as a Computer Operator, eight or nine years later, I was promoted to General Manager of what had become a one-hundred-employee Mainframe Computer Service Bureau. That came from hard work, long hours and a desire to grow, lead and learn including going to night school to earn my Business Management Degree at John Carroll University paid for by C-Trac.

After 10 successful years, surprisingly, the two C-Trac owners decided to get a divorce from each other. And there we were, "x" number of employees who were like kids in a divorce because the parents decided to go their separate ways with the business. It wasn't a good feeling to be at their beck and call "Do I go with Mom, or do I go with Dad?" It taught me a lesson that you've got to have a "Plan B." If you rely on one thing or one company or one situation, it can fall on you like a ton of bricks. That's where I instilled within me and I still share to this day with people I mentor that it's a good idea to have some kind of "Plan B" in place.

I found my way forward in BDPA

So there I was, on the west side of Cleveland which was very segregated with Whites living on this side of Lake Erie while Blacks lived on the east side. I felt like I was the only black person out there, as an orphan if you will, with no network. I didn't know anybody outside of this company. My wife at the time, Anita, suggested I talk to our neighbor, Sandra Noble, who had told us about a group that she was a part of called "The Black Data Something." That was the start of my involvement with BDPA in 1987 under the leadership of Ken Wilson the Cleveland Chapter President. Becoming a DP orphan was my motivation to join BDPA to meet some other black folks in the computer industry. Did I ever!

Then I stepped up into a leadership role

I remember my first job in the Cleveland Chapter was kind of forced on me by Carol (Peacock) Johnson. There was a position open for Program Chairperson and Carol, who I didn't know at the time, turned around and said, Why not you?" So I put my hand up and became Program Chair with the responsibility for identifying speakers and topics for our Monthly Program Meetings. I've been told, it was a year of outstanding programs and events toward a great start with BPDA and it was a great time. It helped to establish my new network of contacts in the community by inviting them to speak at our session. This was step one to expand my network and connections in Cleveland.

Step two was attending my first BDPA National Conference in Los Angeles. I'll jump ahead to the Saturday night banquet where the Detroit Chapter won every other national award that was given out that night. I remember their President, Dianne Davis, walking up to the podium many times to pick up a trophy. That sparked my competitive juices that, "If Detroit can do it, Cleveland can do it." So it became somewhat of a friendly competition as I looked at it. Detroit, Chicago and New York were the top chapters of the early 90s. Cleveland was hanging in there but that's what motivated me to service and leadership and why I ultimately became the Cleveland Chapter President in 1990. I wanted to go "toe to toe" with those guys and gals on who can be the best BDPA chapter in the country.

We never knocked them off, (Chicago followed Detroit in the years to come) but we came in second a couple of years with the Cleveland Chapter making an impact during the early to mid-90s. It was truly a friendly competition, fostered by helping in the community and being able to "talk trash" about helping and teaching others about DP with our peers in other cities where my network was growing outside of Cleveland. It provided great memories and the motivation for continued leadership, sponsorship and friendship.

Moving into Sales and Marketing

My first major career move to sales was somewhat forced on me or I fell into it. At C-Trac, we offered services consisting of Inventory Control and Accounting programs in a batch process. My job at the time was to manage the internal mainframe operations, understand the software, train customers and to get their data reports back to them on a timely basis. In the course of doing that, I learned the software inside out.

The company always had trouble finding salespeople that could sell and also understand inventory control principals which wasn't one of the most popular services as a career back then, but, it's an important foundation for any business. The next thing I knew, I was asked to consider moving into sales. And that led to the decision to go to work with "Mom," after the owners decided to split the company up. "Dad" wanted to remain a Computer Service Bureau on the Mainframe while "Mom" wanted to move the software off the Mainframe to something called a Minicomputer which meant our customers had to buy their first computer in order to run the software on it. So it created an opportunity for me to learn about minicomputers in the integration of software and hardware to provide a total solution for clients.

That's how I transitioned from DP operations into computer software sales. It was a specific niche market, servicing the material handling industry (lift trucks and tow motors) to help track inventory of thousands of parts and service hours.

So here I am in 1985, young black guy traveling around the country for the first time, walking into lift truck dealerships, meeting these all-white small businesses. The owners were sharks, tough businesspeople that had no clue about minicomputers. So I had to figure out how to interact and relate with them. I did that through knowing the software, knowing what I was talking about and having a great mentor at the time, Bob Walters, who could talk birds out of a tree.

Bob had a style and persona that made you want to listen to him. I picked up on his skills which were pretty successful at selling minicomputers to lift-truck dealers around the country.

Minicomputers led me to an opportunity that came up from a BDPA member in Detroit named Tony Adams, a Human Resources Manager for the Digital Equipment Company (DEC). They had a mandate to hire black professional salespeople. So next thing I know, I'm working for DEC, a Fortune 500 company and number two competitor to IBM, selling DEC Minicomputers across the country to Fortune 500 companies. DEC was headquartered in Boston, where training took place. I was at the Beachwood Ohio office with quite a few other BDPA members over my eight years there.

Sales vs. Tech Sales Support

In retrospect, the first half of my data processing career, on mainframe computers, I developed skills in operations, manage people and deliver services. This evolved to customer service and training. I had to be the, quote unquote, expert because I was in front of an audience of people who wanted to learn about computers and application software.

In sales, what I came to learn was you had to be a good listener to allow people to tell you their problems and to share how their business operates.

That became my secret weapon. I listened with the knowledge that I got the software in my head and I listened for how to best make that connection at the right time. In sales, you don't want to deliver a message prematurely, or tell a customer how great your computer is when you don't know what their problems are.

So a big part of what I learned was fact gathering, listening and then feeding that information back to them to make sure they knew I understood. I don't think I was a big "closer," because I waited for the client to make the decision that it was time to buy my solution to their problems. I let them close themselves by answering their concerns and questions. I used to have a motto that, "People will buy from you if you let them."

Speaking to Young BDPA Members

If I were speaking at a BDPA Meeting today to young people, members, or prospective BDPA members, I would talk about "Purpose and Growth." That in order to find purpose and growth, personally, you have to give of yourself, first and foremost.

You have to put the time in. You have to volunteer to be the Program Chairperson for example. You have to volunteer to pick up the high school kids for the computer competition. You have to give first and in that giving you find purpose. In finding purpose, you grow and within that growth your network grows through the association of membership and through learning about people while listening to their story of how they got to be where they are and what their challenges are.

So, you've got to give, you've got to listen and you can't expect anything in return while you're giving. While you're giving, you can't get. Yours will come later when it's time. When it's time to talk about a promotion at your job; or to make a recommendation; or when it's time to interview at a new company. .

I'll never forget a statement in a national BDPA board meeting by Sheila McCaskill from the Chicago Chapter. I'm going to paraphrase a little bit, but she said, "After what we go through in BDPA with each other, the rest of the world is easy."

I carry that statement with me to this day because we had some battles in BDPA. I say that lovingly and positively. We carry those experiences into the real world based on purpose, growth and the camaraderie of BDPA.

I think one of the most important skills one can have is to understand how to build consensus. I think that's an important attribute that everyone should strive for because we are different people coming from different places and backgrounds and scenarios. How do we bring all that information and talent together toward a common purpose? You have to have consensus, right? And I've learned that through BDPA.

I can recall board meetings, sitting around a large conference room with forty chapter presidents talking about an issue or situation and "How do we address it?" My role and responsibility was to try to organize that into a common direction. So building consensus and the ability to listen and share was essential. At the same time, you have to move the conversation to conclusion. Consensus building is one thing and it takes a lot of effort, but you've got to find consensus in order to go forward.

Accomplishments in BDPA

In 1995-96, Perry Carter from the Washington, D.C. Chapter came up with a plan to do something called "email," which he brought to BDPA while I was National President. We agreed to sign up with the first black Internet Service Provider which was introduced as "US Black Online." I felt great about that and I have fond memories of BDPA having its own email system.

The second thing was introducing a strategic plan which called for significant change in how the national organization operated.

Following months of strategic and tactical planning the Enterprise Transformation Plan (ETP) was developed which provided a total review of how BDPA operates internally, what our goals were, what our objectives are and what was needed to change or adjust to prepare for the future.

ETP was presented to the BDPA National Board of Directors in Houston, Texas in 1997. It was discussed, voted on and adopted to move forward by assigning Vice Presidents to head up Membership, Education and Finance to provide accountability and responsibility. ETP also provided the internal structure underneath to support their leadership. As far as I know, ETP remains the operational foundation for BDPA today.

Lastly, in 1996, I was introduced to a team from the Chicago Chapter that had started a senior management group of African-American Chief Technology Officers (CTOs) and Chief Information Officers (CIOs). Together we developed a plan for that group to mentor BDPA members and provide connectivity between the Executive IT professional and the up-and-coming Programmer, Operator or Developer. That year ITSMF and BDPA came together at the National Conference in Atlanta to begin a very productive and reciprocal relationship. I was honored to be a part of the original organizing team and was my pleasure to deliver to National BDPA.

Nowadays

With the evolution to the Internet in 1999-2000, I recognized it was time for me to evolve from data processing and information technology. Although I have transitioned, I still follow BDPA and take pride in that continuation. I've watched that evolution and marvel at the young talent, opportunities and technology enhancements that are at their fingertips. There is no limit to what BDPA can achieve.

I am now working in financial services helping families and those planning for retirement. I am also an elected Council Representative in Mayfield Village Ohio where I am the only African-American on Council. I guess somethings still remain the same and there is still a lot of work to be done.

Margaret (Midge) Johnson

CHAPTER 9

Margaret (Midge) Johnson

Margaret "Midge" Johnson is a retired IT Professional after 52 years in the industry. She is currently working her home based business, MEJ Helps, LLC, that helps people in numerous beneficial ways. Ms. Johnson has earned a Bachelor of Business Administration degree in Management and Operations from Bowie State University, and a Master's in Public Administration with a Specialization in Systems Analysis from the University of Southern California Extension in D.C. During her extensive career, she worked for several consulting companies, on a numerous government contracts, including with Booz Allen Hamilton, where she was a preeminent Project Manager and Systems Analyst, completing her career at GEICO as a Senior Systems Analyst. For BDPA, Midge has served in several essential roles, including Washington D.C. Chapter President in 1986, National Conference Committee Member, and becoming the first BDPA National Executive Director in 1991.

In a January 23, 2021 interview, Midge talked about life, her career, and BDPA.

Be a Team Player

By Margaret (Midge) Johnson

I was born in Gadsden, Alabama in 1943, and was raised in Gadsden until my family migrated to Ohio in 1954. It's mind-boggling: I've traveled so very far to where I am today, that all I can say is "Oh my God." When I got in Cleveland, I went to Doan Elementary, on East 105th Street. And because I came from the South, they immediately wanted to put me back a grade; they assumed that since I came from the South, I couldn't be as smart as the rest. My mother being the person she was, went up to the school, and "went off," because believe it or not, in Alabama, I could read and write at the age of four because we were taught early. And when my mom went to the school, she said, "My daughter knows more than anybody you have from the fourth grade, ask her anything" and they did. My mother was right. I knew more than the rest of them because I was taught earlier. So they allowed me to stay in the right grade, which was like, "Oh, my goodness."

I attended Addison Jr. High School, then East High School (The Mighty Blue Bombers) where I graduated in 1961. During all three years at East High, I played clarinet in the marching band. Interestingly enough, marching band was not my first choice. I wanted to be a cheerleader, but at that time, East High was predominantly white, and only one fair-skinned black girl, at a time, was allowed on the cheerleading team. No one has ever mistakenly called me fair skinned. So I decided, "Well, if I can't be a cheerleader, I'll join the marching band," and that's what I did. In band, orchestra, and ensembles, I played the E-flat, B-flat, Alto, and Bass Clarinets. When I battled in two woodwind-quartet competitions, I finished first, then second. And in spite of the fact that my folks couldn't afford private lessons, I practiced on my own; staying after school to practice because my dad wouldn't let me bring that "loud noise" home.

Blacks weren't getting promoted at all

After graduating from high school, I earned an Associate's degree in Business Management with a minor in Data Processing at Cuyahoga Community College. But even with Data Processing degree as a minor, they wouldn't let us—black folks—move up into the higher-paying jobs. We had the same training from Cuyahoga Community College as the white guys, but they weren't promoting us to Programmer or Manager positions. So I worked as a Keypunch Operator until I eventually got into a training program at a company in Cleveland called Diamond Shamrock. I did that until I got married, and my husband got transferred to the D.C. area, Maryland. So, when we moved to Maryland, my kids said moving was the best thing that could have happened to them, because in D.C. metro, they got to see a completely different world than the world they experienced growing up in Cleveland.

As soon as we got in our new house, before we even unpacked, I drove to Bowie State University so I could enroll in courses to complete my bachelor's degree. After completing that, I went to a University of Southern California (USC) university extension in D.C., which was mostly attended by military and federal government people. At USC, I got my Masters in Public Administration with a specialization in Systems Analysis.

Then I worked for several consulting companies on government contracts though I never worked directly for the government except one job for two years at the Federal Reserve Board (The Fed). And in all honesty, I left "The Fed" because the racial inequality there was blatant, systemic, and rampant. I was capable of doing a lot more than I was permitted to do, but blacks weren't getting promoted at all.

So, I left there and went to Booz Allen Hamilton (Booz Allen). And this is where I met a young lady named Linnie Frank who told me about an organization called BDPA. I said, "What is that?" She said, "Black Data Processing Associates." And I said, "Okay, what are you all doing?" And she told me about how Earl Pace started BDPA. And I said, "Well, I'd like to go to a meeting." And I did, and I joined; not knowing fully what it was about. But I knew it was for me. I joined in 1984, and from that point on, I was actively involved in the D.C. chapter until 1991 when I became the first National Executive Director.

Vivian C. Wilson

Vivian Wilson was one of BDPA's great National Presidents. And interestingly enough, Vivian and I met when we were 15 years old in Cleveland. But back then, she was Clara Cannon, because her maiden name was Cannon, and her family called her by her middle name, Clara. We had met because her sister and my mom worked together, but we lost track of each other after I moved to Maryland.

Then, in 1984, God allowed our paths to cross again. That year, the National Conference was in Cleveland: Vivian was the National Conference Coordinator, and I was the Conference Coordinator for the D.C. Chapter. So they gave me Miss Wilson's name, but at the time, I didn't know who Miss Wilson was; I knew Clara Cannon. So I called Miss Vivian Wilson, and told her who I was, and that I was the conference contact person for the D.C. Chapter, and wanted to know what we could do, how could I help, and all that kind of stuff. And after we talked BDPA for maybe half an hour, I moved the conversation in a more personal direction:

"I used to live in Cleveland," I revealed.

"Where'd you go to school?" She asked.

"East High. Where'd you go to school?" I asked.

"John Adams."

"Oh, I used to have a friend that went to John Adams named Clara Cannon."

"That's me!"

"It says Vivian Wilson."

"I'm Clara Cannon, but you were Margaret Small when I met you."

"That's my maiden name."

So, we talked for an hour and a half, recommitted our friendship, and we were constantly in communication with each other until the day she transitioned.

Becoming an IMS Database Expert

As mentioned earlier, I left the Federal Reserve because their racism was holding me back. But I also left "The Fed" because a major consulting firm—Booz Allen Hamilton—offered me a more attractive position that allowed me to be the expert that I had become at designing IMS databases. So through Booz Allen, I worked as a consultant for seven or eight different government agencies, and on every consulting engagement, I was always the database designer. And any time something new came out, they kept me current in the technology. I became knowledgeable in several projects, designs, specifications, and requirements.

But later on, they started treating me as "less than" my white-male coworkers, so I started looking for another position. And when I got a job-offer letter from another consulting firm, I went to the Senior Vice President at Booz-Allen, and said, "I am giving you my resignation. I have a job to go to." He said, "What? Why?" I said, "I'm going to another job, because I'm working like a dog, working half the night, doing all the database-design work, and you don't give me a raise like I deserve, and I don't have to take that. Here's my resignation letter." And I let them see it. And at that moment he called his secretary and told him to clear his calendar for the rest of the day. And he took me to lunch, and at lunch I said, "I can't play your games. You promised I'd be compensated, but I'm not, so I'm going." He said, "Okay, okay, okay! What if we give you a raise?" I said, "Put it in writing". And he called HR and told them, "Give Midge Johnson a raise immediately." They gave me a decent raise, and I became Project Manager for all the new projects. So I stayed at Booz-Allen for a few more years until I left for a better opportunity at another consulting firm up in Baltimore, working on a contract with the Health Care Financial Administration (HCFA). They were associated with Social Security, and I worked at that consulting firm for three years as a Project Manager until the contract ended.

So I called my old manager at Booz Allen, and he offered me a $15 thousand raise to come back, and promised that I would never again have to work crazy hours, or write any crazy last-minute proposals. So his offer and promises convinced me to go back to Booz Allen to work on a Health and Human Services database project. But when I finished that project, and they didn't promote me, I left them for good.

And believe it or not, I ended up going to Geico, working on "Y2K" projects, because they had IMS database projects and programs, and I could do all those things. So they hired me, and I stayed at Geico until I retired with a 401K account, profit sharing, and a pension.

All this time, I was in BDPA

During the course of doing all of that, throughout my career, I mentored a lot of people, while I was with BDPA. And in 1990, when we hosted the National Conference in D.C., I went to companies to get their backing and sponsorship for the conference. Wayne Hicks said, "You need a PowerPoint." But I said, "No, I don't, because when I go to executives and I talk to them, and they hear the BDPA story, and they hear sincerity and commitment in my voice, I get the money." Now I remember one company in particular,

MCI, who provided phones for all of the kids in the Computer Competition to be able to call home while they were there.

When you talk from the heart, they hear the sincerity, and they hear your commitment to BDPA. They're not blind; they see the inequality, too. So when I talk about how our people didn't get the same career opportunities as our white counterparts, corporate executives are eager to co-sponsor and support our mission.

High School Computer Competition

When I met Dr. Jesse Bemley in 1986, at a D.C. chapter meeting, he suggested that BDPA start a high school computer competition. I was the D.C. Chapter President, and I said, "Okay, what do you want me to do?" He said, "You get the money for me, and I'll get the kids together." So I got the money, he got the kids, and just like that, the BDPA High School Computer Competition was born. At that first "pilot" competition at our 1986 National Conference in Atlanta, we had two teams; D.C. and Atlanta. The D.C. chapter won, and following that success, I became even more involved in expanding our High School Computer Competition program.

When we're speaking to professionals in data processing and information technology, we're speaking to adult audiences. But when we're talking to students, we have to keep in mind that they were born in a different era than we were, and they hear with a different ear than adults do. So as the BDPA student computer competition began to attract larger student audiences, we decided to start a BDPA student chapter that focused on and served the needs of students.

To get us started, I did the initial paperwork; the 501(c)(3), and the nonprofit application to get the Student Chapters up and running. When we finally got the student chapters started, we got much needed help from a gentleman returning from Manchester, England, Louis Hunt who was originally from Toledo, Ohio. He had gone to England to work, and he had returned to the States to the D.C. area, and offered his services to BDPA. I knew him, and knew that he was good at organizing. So he took over, put the student chapters on a solid foundation, and accomplished a lot in the six months we had him with us

Then as the Washington, D.C. chapter started doing more and more with the kids, Jesse Bemley, William Johnson, Perry Carter, Earl Pace, and others were helping other BDPA chapters do more with their students, and they were helping other chapters to start computer competition teams. Before we knew it, almost every chapter in BDPA had a computer competition team, and some were starting student chapters, too.

Executive Director

AJ Cooper, our lawyer, got BDPA some free office space in his law-office building. Meanwhile, I was convincing people who were looking for jobs—who were in between jobs—to work in the office for BDPA. So BDPA had an office, and BDPA had people working in that office during the day, every day. And somewhere along the way, somebody decided we needed an Executive Director. So, I became BDPA's first Executive Director in 1991, and I stayed in that position until 1999.

National Conference Team

Because BDPA was a labor of love, I worked my day job, volunteered in the D.C. chapter, volunteered as Executive Director, and worked on the National Conference team, too. We worked all fifteen BDPA National Conferences from 1984 to 1999. It was amazing how Vivian kept our conference team together, and kept the entire conference-coordination process running like a well-oiled engine for all those years. She selected people for the team who wanted to help people. Whatever needed to be done, and whatever we were assigned to do, we just did it and got it done. People were amazed, but what people didn't know was, we worked all evening and went to bed at 11, 11:30, 12 o'clock at midnight during the conference, and got up at 6:00 a.m. to make sure everything was set up, and in place.

Life After BDPA and Employment

But now that I'm retired, I focus my energy on my church where I'm active on the board of directors, and president of an outreach ministry that's connected to but separate from my church. In the outreach ministry, we go around Maryland ministering to people through the Bible's Holy Word, and through music.

We did all of that before Covid hit. The praise and worship team at my church would go out and sing, partner with other churches, and meet at different places to minister to people who wanted someone to talk to, or wanted to give their life to Christ. We went to Walter Reed Army Medical Center, the Wounded Warriors Section of Bethesda Naval Medical Hospital and other places.

There's a nursing home that we've been ministering to since 2008. We had been going three times a month, but when Covid hit and prevented us from going, they called and asked, "Can you do a virtual ministry?" And that's what we've been doing since the Covid-19 shutdown in March 2020. At the nursing home, they carry an iPad around to each room, and we sing one song for that person, and we pray. And then they take the iPad to another patient, and we sing another song, and we pray. And we've been doing that since May 2020.

I didn't mind doing the tedious stuff. Like when we took Christmas gifts to the nursing homes, I would get all of that stuff; get the boxes, get the tissue, get the cards, and pack it all up. We had one nursing home that had ten residents. We asked them, "What could we get," and they said, "People like music." We said, "Okay." So the vice president asked them, "How would a clock radio be?" They said, "That would be perfect." So we went on the Internet searching, and we found some clock radios for $9.88 at Wal-Mart, and we ordered ten. They were plugins, and they already had backup batteries in them. They were decent, and people at the nursing home were ecstatic. Ten dollars; that was $100 just for ten people. But we spent two hundred dollars for the other place that had over 140 people. We bought small things because we couldn't get them anything like that.

So I'm one of those kind of people who like working behind the scenes; under the radar. I don't have to be up front, and I don't have to be on stage. I get my "Thank You" from God.

Right now, I attend (virtually) Maryland International Tabernacle. We're a non-denominational church, and my Pastor is based in Plainfield, New Jersey. Every morning from 4:30 to 5:30, I get on her prayer line. We go through planned scripture readings in the Bible for the first half hour. Then our Pastor gives exhortations on the scriptures we read, what it means, and how we can apply it in our lives. I had to laugh. They say, "Maryland International," and it is. But I'm one of two people born in the United States. We have people from Jamaica, Trinidad, Nigeria, Sierra Leone, and

Puerto Rico—plus the two of us born in the USA, and that's fine with me.

My virtual church does not prevent me from staying active in my local church. I send out communications, and get people set up on the church and the outreach-ministry websites. We partner with other ministries because scripture teaches us that "No man is an island unto themselves." That means, "Work with each other." Different ministries have unique focuses, but combining two ministries makes both more powerful. We go to where people are, because for a lot of people, going to a church building is simply not something they're going to do. So, unless we go to them, they might never hear our testimonies. When you share your testimony about what God has done for you, it makes people pay attention, and it makes them want to know more (Revelation 12:11). That's outreach.

My Book

Pictured below, my first book, "They Didn't Get That Way By Themselves or a Common Sense/Spiritual Approach to Training Your Child," helps families train children from birth to seven years old. I'm working on my next two books—in a three book set—about training children eight and older.

Midge's book is available on Amazon.

Lessons Learned

Everybody is different. Two people can hear the same words but interpret and process those words differently. Therefore, I learned to confirm a person's interpretation of what I said, or what they said. If you think you heard something one way, you might have to say, "Let me make sure I understand what you're saying," then say what you think they said.

Everybody has something good to offer. Working on different projects, you would have people who were good at one thing, and other people were better at another thing. But when you bring them all together, you got a great project going out. So to me, I never looked at anybody's shortcomings. My biggest shortcoming to you might be a benefit to somebody else, or a plus. I remember on a couple of Booz Allen projects, there were a couple of ladies that were kind of antagonistic toward each other. I took them out of the room, talked to them, and asked them what the problem was. I said, "Let me put it to you this way: You do what you need to do to get your job done, and if you have an issue, let me know, and I'll take care of it." I told them both the same thing, and for some strange reason after that, they didn't argue anymore. If they had an issue or something , they would come to me.

As nice as people think I am, I have another side. But you have to do an awful lot to take me there. So, I always try to keep things calm. Every project that I managed at Booz Allen, and other companies, it worked.

We got the work done. We made all of our deadlines. We didn't miss anything. So it was a mutual respect for one another. If one person was good at doing one thing, let them do what they did well. When would we have presentations and meetings, I basically focused on people strengths; not their weaknesses. We all came together to work, and it made sense. And that's basically how I managed all the projects at my work

In my church and ministry, there are not many issues. Everybody helps set up the equipment out on the street or right on the sidewalk. Everybody pitched in. And that's what I got from BDPA. Everybody pitched in when we were doing conferences and things like that. That's what I carried over to my outreach ministry, even in the church. Even today, I'm on the board of directors for the church. Everybody pitches in. Whatever your strength is, we'll go with it, and we support you, and vice versa.

I had been in BDPA for seven years before I committed to the things of God. I asked Him, “God, why am I here, why am I still here, why am I doing this?” Because I was doing this from 1984 to 1999. What I learned in BDPA, I used in the outreach ministries to this day. Because we deal with people, and people tend to forget we’re human beings first. We’re not the super spiritual beings that we're going to be on the other side. We're human beings and we have human shortcomings and human frailties. And when you ignore them because of your position, you set up problems. So I just I kept going with BDPA, and I learned a lot. And I have to admit working with Vivian and the other women on the team, you know; Vivian, Gerry, Kathy Procope, Twila, Mary Ann, and Cecilia; we all worked well together, and we still keep in contact today. We worked so well together; it was amazing. We just did what we had to do. It was it was an experience I'll never, ever forget. I thank God for that, because I did and said a lot of things that I've learned from BDPA that I use in the ministries.

We are a smart people

We (African Americans) are a smart people, and we can learn and do a lot of things that we've never been given credit for. One of the things that brought that home to me was the movie, "Hidden Figures." I also received a video that was recorded by a white gentleman who offered to tell us about the white people in the bible. After a slight pause, he asked if we were ready for the answer because he didn't want us all to miss the answer. He then stated that **"There were none!"** When you think about Moses, David, Solomon, and many others who were people of color, you come to realize that whole area were people of color because they were near the equator.

When you learn to accept that you're smart, that you have something to offer, something to give, then you don't let anything or anybody make you feel "less than." So when I heard about BDPA, I wanted to be a part of this because I want my people to know how smart they are, and what they can be. I wanted to be one of the cheerleaders. From 1975 to where we are in 2021. Oh my! And we're still going strong.

We were a team

The thing that amazed me a lot is when we really got going with the computer competition, it wasn't just black girls or black kids. It was any culture, any color, we didn't care. I was so impressed with a lot of them, and I went out of my way with the D.C. team when I was President. I would do the special things for them when they had practices, I would show up, encourage them, and bring more. I just made them feel like they were our kids when it came to the computer competition that we were going to take good care of them. At that first one, when we went from D.C. to Atlanta for the first competition in 1986, we realized was that about 75% of kids had never been in a hotel or on a plane or out of the city. So we said, "Okay, we're going to have to help them out." We had people who would be guardians and chaperones at the conference, watching rooms and watching the stuff that kids tend to do, and I remember that we "yanked up" a few of them. But we tried to give them an opportunity to see a different side of life, and give them something to look forward to. That let us know that some of the students needed help; everybody don't have everything they need. What we did for those kids was go and buy clothes if they didn't have any nice clothes to wear. I'm saying we did what we needed to do to make them feel comfortable. Some of the kids came from schools that had everything, and that happens in churches, too. I finally got to a point where if people don't realize Jesus didn't dress up in a silk shirt and tie when he was out there in the hinterlands ministering the word, why do we want people to have to dress up to come to church? Being clean and covered is what I look for; clean and covered. You don't have to be dressed to the nines. So from dealing with the kids who hadn't been used to much, I started looking at things differently, and I tried to give more. They may not have been exposed to certain things nor learned from their parent or whoever they're living with. Sometimes they need that other person to talk to them, who may see things differently and hopefully help them.

"Teamwork involves a willingness to do whatever the team needs done."

—Midge Johnson

Richard Wayne Hicks, Jr.

CHAPTER 10

R. Wayne Hicks, Jr.

Energize and Inspire People to Win

Wayne Hicks worked his butt off. He was a charismatic achiever — and a fast-talking mover-and-shaker — who pushed for progress—passionately, purposefully, and relentlessly. And continuously, Wayne moved maniacally, almost magically, and always meaningfully, toward a brighter future for himself and the people he loved. Whether Wayne was working with employees at the Internal Revenue Service (IRS), where he was the executive in charge of the Cincinnati Service Center; whether Wayne was mentoring members of the Black Data Processing Associates (BDPA), where he presided over the organization nationally; or whether he was hanging out with friends and family; Wayne was perpetually in motion, until suddenly, on June 7, 2018, R. Wayne Hicks, Jr. passed away peacefully at home.

For more than thirty years, Wayne was a tireless champion of the Black Data Processing Associates (BDPA) and promoting diversity in technology and expanding STEM experiences for youth in underserved communities.

For the last twelve years of his life, Wayne was the Executive Director of the Black Data Processing Associates Education and Technology Foundation (BETF). Prior to that, Wayne was a member of Detroit BDPA, President of Cincinnati BDPA, President of the Cincinnati Business Incubator (2003-2008), and President of National BDPA (2004-2005).

Wayne is survived by his daughters Laura Hicks and Nailah McCloud, son Khalis Hicks, granddaughter Amara McCloud, his mother Elizabeth Hicks, sister Kyra Hicks, and a host of aunts, uncles, cousins, nieces, other family, friends, and colleagues.

But let's go back to the beginning of a great life story.

In Her Own Words

By Elizabeth (Liz) Hicks

In a March 31, 2021 recorded interview, Wayne's mother, Liz Hicks, agreed to share some of her memories of Wayne. This conversation is transcribed and edited for clarity below.

◆

Wayne was born in Los Angeles, California on January 30, 1959. He had a brother Charles, sister Kyra, and a sister Iyisa. So there were two boys and two girls. Wayne was the oldest. The two boys were older, and then the two girls.

He grew up here, and attended Los Angeles Public Schools. When he was in the second grade, he was state-identified gifted academically. And I took him out of the school he was in and put in him the school where I was teaching elementary. He stayed there for a year, and then he was able to go to Castle Heights Elementary School. We didn't call them Magnet schools then, but Castle Heights had full classes of gifted children, and so I was able to get him in there. He did well there, and he made lots of friends. That's one thing Wayne could do: Wayne could make a friend in a minute. He was very, very outgoing.

When he graduated from Castle Heights, and Junior High, we thought he would go to the school where the other Magnet kids had gone, which was Hamilton

High. For some reason, they said he lived out of the district for that school and could not go to Hamilton High. I believe it was racism, and now we know that's what it was. So, he ended up coming back to LA High, which is our school in the neighborhood. He did well there, and his father, Richard Wayne Hicks, Sr., made him know that he was to always take a math class, science class, and history class. All of those academics are what we used to call college prep. Because sometimes the kids would go to school and the counselors would just give them anything. So, his father and I made sure that he had these academic classes. Wayne applied to and was accepted at several colleges.

He really wanted to go to the University of Michigan, but we could not afford that. So he went to University of California, Riverside, and became very involved. In his free time, he would be somewhere playing this pinball game. But kids would stand around and watch him. They called him "The Wiz." I can't remember what they called this pinball game, but you left your score, and Wayne was always up there on the top. Later, he somehow got a radio program at KUCR 88.1 PM, where he played music. Wayne was known as "The Wizard of Soul and Mind." He graduated "Cum Laude."

After graduation, he moved to Detroit, went to work for the IRS, and joined BDPA. He became so involved in BDPA that every other thought in his mind was "BDPA, BDPA." I learned a lot about BDPA just listening to him talk about it.

Detroit is my home. I was so impressed with that chapter, their meetings, and how organized they were. All the Chairs had their reports in writing. Everyone got up; they did what they were supposed to do. I had never been to a meeting like that before in my life. And they were so friendly and so knowledgeable about what they did. Diane Davis was some kind of President!

The other thing that impressed me about BDPA was, they were always dressed. They were always professional. That impressed me because these were young people.

Wayne was called on to speak at that meeting. He was called on to speak at a lot of BDPA chapters. That's when I knew he could speak.

And so, I decided I wanted to join the Detroit Chapter. And Wayne said, "Mama, it's no sense you joining the Detroit Chapter. There's a Chapter in Los Angeles." So he got in touch with someone, and that's how I joined the Los Angeles Chapter. Robert Riddick was the President.

Then Wayne moved to Cincinnati. I don't know what he did in Cincinnati, I just know that he did. Everything I know about Wayne after he left LA, BDPA was involved.

Wayne was a walking commercial for BDPA, but in the most natural way. It was just part of him, because

BDPA was his passion. You've got to have a passion, and I think Wayne would tell kids that as well.

Years later, in 2012, I had to have knee surgery. My kids were now grown, living in different places, and Wayne came out here to Los Angeles and cared for me. The first time he came out and stayed with me almost three months. Always on that computer with BDPA and the Foundation (BETF). I knew the names of every President, whatever the chapter. I don't know what they were talking about, but he spent most of the day doing that. The next year, I had my second surgery, he came back again, he did the same. He worked very hard in that.

BDPA did a job with my son, and made him even more than he would have been.

In Her Own Words

By Shenita Hicks

In a June 28, 2021 recorded interview, Wayne's former wife, Shenita Hicks, agreed to share some of her memories of Wayne. This conversation was transcribed and edited for clarity below.

◆

Wayne and I met while we were both working for the Internal Revenue Service (IRS). At the IRS, Wayne was viewed as a great communicator, an innovator, and someone who was willing to take on a challenge. He always had a passion for the advancement of technology, particularly as it relates to African Americans. He often brought the tenets of BDPA into IRS to try to show some of the interconnections between what BDPA was doing and how that could help IRS, and vice versa.

One of Wayne's early positions in the IRS was in the Equal Employment and Opportunity Office. He became grounded there in terms of a desire to help the advancement of African Americans. Inside the IRS, there is an organization called "Association for the Improvement of Minorities in IRS." Wayne was an active member, and in this organization, he continued his passion for wanting to help others.

Ever since I've known Wayne, he was always involved in BDPA. I think what I remember most about

Wayne and BDPA is; although he was not an IT man by trade who was formally trained in technology or computers, he had this really deep understanding of how technology was going to rule the world, so to speak. He did not shy away from the use of a computer. He could see how technology as a communication vehicle was going to be transformational and how the need to be educated in the use of technology was going to be a career for the future. So he was always trying to position folks around him to be prepared for what the future would bring. His brain was always working. He was always thinking, and when something would hit him, he would get it out quickly, so he could share information with those who needed to know.

He was very involved in technology camps that BDPA has for the young people. He was very interested and involved in trying to equip young people, to introduce them early to different facets of technology. And then there was his competitive spirit in terms of trying to help his team win at competitions. I attended a few of those competitions, and they were very interesting, and the BDPA volunteers were just phenomenal. And over the years, I probably attended a few of the BDPA Program meetings/events at different locations.

If I were speaking to a group of young people about how and why BDPA could benefit them, I would start by telling them, you don't have to have any previous knowledge, interest, or exposure to technology, but you do have to be open to coming into the BDPA space. Allow folks to expose you to it, and teach you the technology, and show you the riches, and show you the opportunities it can create for you. Because technology is driving everything we do, whether you are an IT professional, or not. Many employers will be asking young people about their skills, and so, if you have technology skills in your toolbox, you are a leg up on those who don't. As it relates to deciding to become an IT professional, you're in a perfect space within BDPA to tap into the experience and knowledge of folks who are there; to learn more about what it takes to enter the profession, and learn more about the opportunities for the future.

I hope it goes without saying that Wayne was truly devoted to the principles of BDPA, and to the BDPA organization. We used to joke from time to time that he "bled" BDPA, and if he had to choose between BDPA and something else, he would have to stop and think about it for minute. He really would, because he was there as the organization was continuing to grow and mature, and he had some roles in that growth and maturity. He was kind of like a father who took great pride in watching BDPA evolve. Wayne was committed to BDPA and believed it to be a very worthwhile organization. His vision was to make BDPA a strong global organization.

Martin Luther King III and Richard Wayne Hicks, Jr.

Part III

Pathways to A Brighter Future

Michael D. Robinson

CHAPTER 11

Michael D. Robinson

Michael Robinson's success is the product of hard work, street smarts, and mentorship through organizations like BDPA and BDPA's sister organization, the IT Senior Management Forum (ITSMF). Mr. Robinson is Vice President Healthcare North America for VMware, Managing Partner of MiRo Ventures, LLC, and serves on the Board of Directors of NovoDynamics, Inc. Previously, Michael was Vice President, US Health and Life Sciences for Microsoft, where he was employed fifteen years, Vice President Professional Services for Hitachi Data Systems, where he was employed six years, and Managing Director of the Southeast Consulting Practice for Serling Software, where he was employed six years, and a Director at the New York Telephone Company (NYNEX), where he was employed fifteen years. And educationally, Michael earned an MBA in Management from Pace University, in New York City.

Formed in 1996, from conversations between prominent tech executives, including members of BDPA, the ITSMF positions Black Professionals for Technology Leadership. Under the leadership of Carl Williams, this non-profit professional organization began recruiting Black professionals who ranked among the Who's Who in technology, along with companies and individuals that dared to disrupt the status quo and seek more diversity, equity, and inclusion among technology executives.

In a June 11, 2021 recorded interview, Michael Robinson talked about his career, his life, BDPA, and the ITSMF.

The IT Senior Management Forum

By Michael D. Robinson

My three brothers, my sister, and I came from really humble beginnings. In New York City, in the Bronx, where we grew up, we didn't have a lot of role models we could look up to. No one in my family had attended higher education. My dad had only gone to the ninth grade in high school. And so, I grew up in an environment where higher education was not something I even considered.

I went to Evander Childs High School, then later, after we moved to Westchester County, New York, which was culturally different from the Bronx, I graduated from New Rochelle High School. So I went from a very ethnic environment, to one that was more homogenized. But even within that homogenization, I had very few role models.

And we'll get to this question later, but one of the great things about BDPA and ITSMF, is that they provide those role models for younger people. Incidentally, my younger brother, Kevin Robinson, started the Connecticut Chapter of BDPA.

But that said, I dropped out of high school in my senior year. And the story behind dropping out is that I wanted to play professional football. I was a Cornerback, was pretty quick, had received a Division-1 football scholarship, but found out late in my senior year in high school that I didn't have enough credits to graduate. So I said to myself, "I'll show them," and I quit high school. To round out that story, my dad, who as mentioned, did not have a high school education; my dad came to me and said, "Michael, I've never asked you for anything, but the one thing I asked you to do is make sure that you finish your high school education." So, I was working at the time, and I went to night school and finished my degree.

The Telephone Company

Moving on, I got a job at the local telephone company, as an Installer, installing telephone networks. And a friend of my brother was Chris Sampson—who was one of the most senior African-Americans at the time at the phone company. Chris would see me come in to work in the morning. I would always be early; a work ethic from my parents. And Chris would catch me in the morning and say, "Hey, Michael, there's a bright future in this field called data processing." And at the time, I was working in a technical field, but I was also a Union Rep. So from my perspective, data processing was a management job, and I absolutely did not want a management job, because I was, with overtime, already making more money than most managers, which was more than I had ever envisioned growing up as a young man.

But Chris was relentless, and he rode me for years. Literally, I would see him every day and he finally said to me, "Michael, listen: I won't bother you. Just take the data-processing aptitude exam, and see how you do. You might not even be qualified or have the aptitude to do this. And I said, "All right, Chris. If this gets you off my back, I'll take the test." And so I took the test, and scored really well. And not only did Chris amp up his pursuit of me, but he also enlisted a sister—a BDPA member named Thelma Gaddis—to help push me toward a career in data processing. Thelma ran the training for BDPA's High School Computer Competition team, and she was even more relentless than Chris was in pushing me to get this job. And so finally man, I just said, “Okay man, I'll take the job.”

That's how I started in data processing as a programmer at the phone company. I ended up spending fifteen years there, and I progressed through the organization, got up to the director rank, and right before my career was interrupted by Uncle Sam, I was running a pretty large organization.

Around 1974, I went into the military, and served six years in the United States Marine Corps; two years of active duty, two years in active reserves, and two years inactive reserves. And this was my plan: I wanted to get the GI Bill to fund my education, and those funds would supplement the tuition reimbursement that you got at the telephone company. So, I came out, started my education, and pursued, an undergraduate degree that took me 30 years to get, but my college education started there.

I spent fifteen years at the phone company, and just before I left, they were going to put me into a management development program where you were guaranteed a vice-president level position. They would get you a graduate degree; I could go to any school in New York that I wanted, and get a graduate degree. But the catch was; I didn't have an undergrad degree at the time.

And so Columbia, NYU, and the likes, they were like, “No thanks.” But one school, Pace University, actually agreed to accept me into their MBA program.

I moved to Atlanta

But I had some personal challenges: I got a divorce and my wife moved to Atlanta. So I made the decision to quit my job and move to Atlanta. And back in the 1980s, after investing fifteen years in one organization, like New York Telephone, and then quitting; that was crazy, and when I told my mother I was quitting, she looked like she was going to have a heart attack. She's like, "No, that's a good job. You're supposed to stay."

So anyway, that's the story of how I started in data processing, beginning with a solid 15-year foundation at the phone company. Then late in 1989, contrary to my mother's admonitions, I left New York, moved to Atlanta, and ended up spending eleven years there before moving to Washington, DC, moving to Dubai, in the United Arab Emirates, then eventually moving back to Manhattan.

Before I moved to Atlanta, I began participating in BDPA

Looking back, it was in the mid-eighties when I met New York BDPA Chapter President, George Baker. And when I attended BDPA meetings, I was really impressed with the focus and the mission of the organization. Although in our business, in the phone company, we had really good representation in BDPA back then in terms of black and brown folks in senior-level positions. There was a brother there named John Graham who actually grew up with Lou Alcindor (Kareem Abdul Jabbar), who was one of the senior directors in our organization. So at the time I joined BDPA, there were at least five or six black directors, working in our IT organization at the phone company, who were already participating in BDPA.

At BDPA, I appreciated the connectedness to building community, building careers, and striving to achieve the broader mission of making sure that we increase the level of our representation and impact in the information technology (IT) industry.

You may have heard the expression, "You can't be what you can't see." And that applies to my statement about coming from humble beginnings, because where I came from, I could not "see" until Chris, Thelma, and others in BDPA helped me see the possibilities of what my career could actually be. And in BDPA, you could see people, who looked like you, working in every facet of the industry, and you could shape your career around the experiences of BDPA members who had already been there and done that.

We did some great things in terms of just making kids aware, and creating events where families could come. And those kinds of activities were what drove me to participate to the extent that in 1988, I ran for and was elected New York BDPA Chapter President.

Not coincidentally, the very next year, the New York Chapter won Chapter of the Year.

IT Senior Management Forum (ITSMF)

I think, as I said before, representation matters, and it matters at senior levels in organizations, that's how change gets implemented into policy. So, we need programs and initiatives to help us develop senior managers that look like us at the Chief Information Officer (CIO) level, and at the C-Suite Board levels of organizations. And I think it's important that, not only do we have representation, but we should also hold people accountable to making a difference as well. And part of that is education, part of that involves getting opportunities for hands-on experiences, and part of that involves relationship building. And both BDPA and ITSMF do all of those things.

I had a conversation with Michael McCrimmon, who was a BDPA member and an ITSMF member as well. And the way Michael put it to me was, "You don't have to make a choice between BDPA and ITSMF; the organizations complement each other. And it's a two way street; the ITSMF benefits from your leadership experiences, too."

The ITSMF organization was a couple of years old when I joined in 1998. I was at Hitachi at the time when we actually hosted a meeting for ITSMF. I was out of touch at the time. And the people I connected with were people that I came to admire and respect. And they have a moniker for that now. They call it "It's my family." My closest friends are part of the

ITSMF organization; people that I've come to rely on, including business advisors. And many of them are still in that organization today.

The connection between BDPA and ITSMF still has an opportunity to meld better, because essentially, the missions of BDPA and ITSMF are the same. I don't know why, or for what reason that hasn't happened over the decades. But there's still an opportunity for us to become more closely aligned.

Ultimately, the mission of ITSMF is important because it provides a safe space for executives to be able to share information and help each other grow. Because once you get to certain levels, the darts come faster and more furiously, people come at you faster and more furiously, and the organization relies on you to get corporate-wide work accomplished through team building and delegation of tasks to your team.

So you need to know more than your technical area of expertise; you also need to know how to motivate, organize, and get work done through other people. And in ITSMF, members get the opportunity to learn from executives who've been there, done that, and more importantly, who look like you, empathize with you, and are committed to helping you succeed.

And in building a pipeline of talent from the classroom to the boardroom, we, in BDPA and ITSMF, have to have some cohesiveness in strategy and execution as we pursue our mutual career, community, and corporate aims.

Mentor Protégé Program

The Mentor Protégé Program started with the recognition that there is a need to build a bridge between folks that are aspiring to go from mid-level management, and get into senior management.

So it started out as a protégé program to help that community, specifically in terms of building skills, making that transformation, and connecting with mentors that help protégés grow professionally.

Since the Mentor Protégé Program was originally launched, we've established three new programs:

1. We added an Academy for Women, exclusively for women, in the mid-level to senior management ranks;

2. We established a Management Academy, which is the evolution of the original Protégé Program; And

3. We established an Executive Management Academy, which is focused on mid-level managers that are aspiring to get to Senior VP and C-level positions.

Moreover, all three of these programs were established with the aim of helping people build the skills to get into the upper echelons of senior management.

And just last week, I gave the keynote for the Mentor Protégé Program graduation. Robert Dixon has been actively involved in that, and Robert Scott actually runs all three of those academies for ITSMF.

Creating Generational Wealth

One of the things I feel like we missed over these last three or four decades is the focus on how do you, not only grow in corporate America, but also, "How do we create generational wealth through entrepreneurship?" And when I look at people like Earl Pace, and Ken Wilson, we really had a number of people who were modeling that entrepreneurship, that I don't feel like we took full advantage of it in terms of the opportunity to grow and build generational wealth. And so that's a challenge that I'm making to ITSMF now, and they're embracing more of the entrepreneurship as a programmatic piece of their business initiatives. When we look at people like David Steward, who created the billion-dollar corporation, "Worldwide Technologies," we should be emulating those types of successes, so that we can be growing, cultivating, and harvesting an entire landscape of entrepreneurs and wealth builders in BDPA, ITSMF, and beyond.

So a number of people like myself, Elaina Robinson, Cedric Nash, Larry Quinlan, have all gotten together, and we put together what we're calling the "Black Summit," that's going to happen this year, and it's about how do we create generational wealth for people. Because, through the hard work of BDPA and ITSMF, a lot of us have accumulated wealth, and have attained positions that we never thought possible. Now, how do we take that wealth and make that wealth generational. How do we focus our people on the strategies that we employ? how do we make sure that that we create opportunities for generational wealth, and take it to the next level? We've got a number of people moving through the pipeline, but how do we make sure that we have a high level of influence and impact?

From my perspective, when we look at diversity, equity and inclusion, representation matters, yes, but influence and impact matters more. And fortunately or unfortunately, we live in a capitalist society, and green is the most important color. So, as we accumulate and manage generational wealth, the representation piece gets solved as well.

In ITSMF, we became close

There are too many people to list in terms of who has helped and influenced me, but I'll tell you this: ITSMF has an initiative called "Check In," where members sit down, get in a circle, and I believe CurVie Burton started this, and you talk about what's going on in your life, what's going on from a business perspective, and as you talk, other people listen. I felt a strong human connection throughout that process.

In one of those sessions, a member was sharing his experiences, and as I listened, I decided, "I'm going to keep my personal stuff to myself," because I was a high school dropout who didn't graduate from an Ivy League college. Nonetheless, this member was totally transparent, open, and raw about his situation; where he was, what was going on in his life, and the challenges he faced. And he convinced me, I needed to open up, be transparent, ask for help, and trust that people have my best interests at heart. So, that was a revelation for me in terms of trusting, opening up, asking for help, and growing.

And it's always been a challenge that, as our organizations grow, "Can we maintain a high level of intimacy and support?" Because through that intimacy and support, we find human connections with people in different ways. My very best friend in the world is Larry Quinlan, who I met in ITSMF. Larry is the CIO for Deloitte. And there are dozens of other people in ITSMF that are very close.

Through BDPA and ITSMF, I grew up again, as I did in my youth, growing up in rough environments, learning who I could and could not trust. And I've learned, over the years, to trust the people in my inner circles, and BDPA and ITSMF is two such circles of trust.

Be great now!

The theme of my keynote at the ITSMF graduation was "Be Great Now!" Because, a lot of times, whether it's cultural, whether it's "imposter syndrome," or just lack of confidence, we sometimes feel like we have to "check all the boxes" even as others are getting a free ride, relatively speaking. Or conversely, we show them—those in power— that we have "checked all the boxes," completed all of the specified prerequisites, and they use that against us, as if we weren't savvy enough to skip some of the steps.

But I feel like NOW is the time when we have to be enlightened and empowered, and say to ourselves, "This is our time to be great—right now." And ultimately, this affirmation requires that we believe in ourselves; our self-worth, skills, and capabilities.

I tell this to people, and I've told this to my kids that, I've never worried about losing a job, I've always felt like I will either be an entrepreneur (as I have several times), or I will be able to secure a better opportunity than the one I left (as I also have several times). And that level of audacity requires confidence and focus, and it requires that you use the skills that you have in transferable ways to opportunities that are different from your current and previous situations.

As mentioned, I grew up in "the hood" where survival skills were important. And some of the tactics that I used to survive in the hood, are applicable in corporations and boardrooms. And being able to understand, recognize, and execute those transformations is important.

As a people, we can no longer wait for others to acknowledge us, or wait for somebody else's blessing or validation. We have to be great—now.

Most Cherished Accomplishments

I'm very proud of my tenure in BDPA, and I never take one hundred percent credit for anything, because the power of BDPA is in the level of collaboration that occurs. But I was one of the architects of the BDPA Education and Technology Foundation (BETF), working with Wayne Hicks. BETF was birthed out of our vision for creating an entity that connected to younger people, and helped further education. Wayne Hicks lifted BETF to higher heights, but I was in the right place at the right time to help get the ball rolling.

And I cherish the transformation our New York chapter made during the time I was President. We took the great accomplishments George Baker had achieved, and we lifted them to the next level. We grew the membership, we got people focused, we engaged the black community, and in recognition of our accomplishments, we won the Chapter of the Year award, and our High School Computer Competition team won the first place trophy. So that was a double bonus.

In ITSMF, I created the gala that they did this year. I challenged the organization to expand our presence and put on a gala that would raise awareness, support, and a significant amount of money. And we were successful in making all of that happen on a shoestring budget.

And the thing I'm most proud of is—and I mentioned earlier, my parents weren't educated—I got to endow a scholarship in their names, and the "Peter and Edith Robinson Scholarship" is an ongoing commitment that ITSMF awards at its gala every year.

Life Lessons I've Learned

The first life lesson is: I don't care how talented or smart you are, you cannot do it by yourself; you have to have a network to be successful. And that network needs to be cultivated over time so that it revolves around people you trust; people who are not just going to say "Yes" to you, but will say what really needs to be said to help you grow and develop. That's absolutely critical. And going back to our culture, it does take a village to continue to grow. And one of the biggest mistakes that people make is they may feel like, "Hey, if I just work hard, then success will take care of itself." But 99 times out of 100, you are not going to succeed without family, friends, teachers, associates, and a professional network that continues to grow as you grow. And that's probably the most critical lesson to learn.

The second one is: You have to be confident in your ability and grow that confidence through acquisition of knowledge, new skills, etc. But to do that, you need to cultivate your curiosity. An intellectual curiosity—a thirst for knowledge—fuels and drives your ambition to create, innovate, and accomplish things. And that involves being curious about ways of the world, and that involves formulating your hypotheses of "What will the future look like, and how can I have impact, and make things better? What did I do today that I shouldn't have, or what can I do tomorrow that will make me better than today?" And so, having that curiosity about growing, developing, creating impact, and improving current situations in your world, is the second most critical lesson to learn, in my humble opinion.

And I think an important distinction here is that you network to build relationships. You don't necessarily network to a particular end. You network to build relationships because you never know when those relationships will either add value or be ones that that you're going to rely on.

And one of the things I got this from my dad is, you treat everybody with respect. So in every organization we're in, we should treat everyone with respect; from the admins to the janitorial staff, you treat people like people.

Technology Around the World

As a technologist, I believe that everybody else is a technologist too, regardless of what you do for a living. Technology lives everywhere, all over the world, and the technology industries might be the greatest industries for anyone to work in. They affect almost every other industry, activity, or issue; whether we're talking about health care, retail, climate change.

Technology is in the mix, and often is at the heart of that industry, activity, or issue. So, it is essential that the members of technology organizations are effective communicators of technologies, and effective implementers of technologies.

Working for Microsoft, I spent five years abroad in the Middle East and Africa working with technology. And that experience opened my eyes to how globally applicable information technologies really are. You'd have some of the richest countries in the world looking at artificial intelligence, and some of these other whiz bang technologies.

One of the projects I worked on that I was most proud of was in Senegal, they had a remote village that we, at Microsoft, helped put online. Senegal had landline communication links in Dakar, the capital city of Senegal, but they had nothing operable connecting the village. So to register births and deaths, the village people would have to travel 100 miles to Dakar to do it. And using an old, antiquated phone line they already had out there, we put a very simple solution in place—that utilized new communication technology that more efficiently utilized that line—that allowed them now to be connected to Dakar via that same phone line. After we put that upgrade in place, they didn't have to travel a hundred miles to record deaths and births. So something as simple as that, a technology we take for granted here, was profoundly life changing there, in that community.

So Microsoft was my 15-year career, after my 15-year career at the phone company, and entrepreneurial and corporate things in between, including where I am today at MiRo Ventures and VMware.

And future is wide open in terms of what technology can do. And the opportunity to change the world and do good things for people is why I focus on health care, both in my personal investment strategies at MiRo Ventures, LLC, and in my day job as Vice President Healthcare North America at VMware. Tech for good, so to speak.

Microsoft's a great company. I love the aspiration, the mission that they had in terms of changing the world one person at a time, and having people live to their full potential. And I remain inspired having met some great leaders there, including, I had the privilege to work with Bill Gates and Steve Ballmer. I think the current CEO, Satya Nadella, has taken the organization to a whole new level, and actually has changed the image of Microsoft from the "evil empire" to something more loved and aligned. And again, the things that they're doing in the cloud, around artificial intelligence, and machine learning, and those kinds of things, I think it's phenomenal. They will continue to be an innovator, I'm proud that I spent 15 years in that organization in some pretty impactful roles. I just mentioned my favorite one, the five years running Middle East and Africa was my favorite.

I lived in Dubai, and I traveled throughout the Middle East and Africa. In fact, I've been to every country in the Middle East except Yemen, and I've traveled to 35 countries in Africa as well.

And ultimately, these amazing experiences, meeting and helping some amazing people around the world, might not have been possible without the help of some amazing people I met in BDPA.

Perry Carter

CHAPTER 12

Perry Carter

Earl G. Graves, Sr., the media mogul who inspired four generations of African Americans to build wealth through entrepreneurship, career advancement and money management, published the first issue of Black Enterprise Magazine in August 1970. Perry Carter, a media prodigy, and a pioneer of the Black Data Processing Associates (BDPA) published the first issue of "*bdpatoday*" Magazine in May 2007. And while Earl Graves became a millionaire mogul, Perry Carter—for 38 years of service to BDPA—has become a mogul in the minds and hearts of hundreds of young people he continues to inspire via the "*bdpatoday*" social-media platform.

A friendly, likeable workaholic, Perry has served BDPA in several other key roles. He was National BDPA's first webmaster, launching "*bdpa.org*" in 1996. He served on BDPA's Board of Directors as National Communications Chair. He helped form, charter and support BDPA chapters in Baltimore, Northern Virginia (NoVA), Hampton Roads, and Huntsville, Alabama. He is the Executive Producer of Popular Technology (PTTV) and founder of the DC chapter's Tablets For Teens program.

Perry's corporate resume is equally extensive, and it includes serving as Vice President and Regional CIO for Tec-Masters, Inc.

And if that weren't enough, Perry currently serves as President of BDPA's Washington, D.C. Chapter.

In an April 14, 2021, recorded interview, Perry talked about his life, his career, and BDPA.

Build Tomorrow Today

By Perry Carter

When I started out as a "Paper Boy" in Philadelphia at age fourteen, I was already fascinated by the publishing industry—news, content, and delivery. In fact, my elementary-school classmates may remember when we were in third and fourth grades, me and a handful of other students would clip pictures and stories from Life, Ebony, Boys Life, and Jet magazines. Then we would put them together into our own magazine re-creations for the pleasure and entertainment of our classmates. And being resourceful third and fourth graders, we used notebook paper for the magazine pages, and manila folders for our magazine covers. Later this month I am actually going back to my elementary school in Philadelphia for a virtual Career Awareness Day where I will share that same story.

Getting up at "Zero Dark Thirty" in the morning and delivering the *Philadelphia Bulletin* newspaper was my first part-time job. This employment occurred in junior high school and then into Central High School.

For those who might not know, Central High in Philadelphia is a college-preparatory school where—to be admitted—you had to pass an entrance exam. Colleges from all over America—and the military—heavily recruited Central's students most of whom matriculated directly into a college or university. But I detoured away from directly entering college because I decided instead to enlist in the United States Air Force, spending almost three years in Colorado Springs, Colorado at the United States Air Force Academy's Preparatory School, and the United States Air Force Academy—prior to my enlistment into the United States Marine Corps.

U.S. Marine Corps

I enlisted in the United States Marine Corps, working as a Reservist while attending Temple University where I earned a Marine Corps-Option Naval ROTC scholarship that allowed me to obtain my education while pursuing a career as an officer in the United States Marine Corps. During that time, I was a double major at Temple University, in Computer Science and Political Science. Upon graduation, I received a commission and became a Data Systems Officer with the Marines. I went to Quantico, Virginia for training at The Basic School for new Marine Officers followed by orders to Computer Sciences School (CSS). My first assignment upon CSS graduation was to the Corps' Central Design and Programming Activity (MCCDPA).

I had two tours in Northern Virginia and the Washington, D.C. area where I was a Software Quality Assurance (SQA) Analyst, and the Deputy Finish Line Operations Officer for the Marine Corps Marathon. The marathon assignment involved real-time data capture and collection via bar codes from all runners who made it to our finish line. And it involved the preparation of custom reports for media, newspapers, and sports magazines.

All of this occurred before the "Internet," before Facebook, and before Windows. We successfully uploaded data from Finish-Line Ops, and migrated that data to mainframe computers using PC Focus (and other software), then we produced the final "greenbar" reports using COBOL.

The Marathon was a high-visibility event with no margins for error. As many may know, the Marines have two major programs for public affairs and public outreach: The Marine Corps Marathon and Toys-for-Tots.

My other active duty assignment sent me to Headquarters Marine Corps (HQMC) in their Manpower branch, where I supported the "Enlisted Assignment (Computer) Model" (EAM). EAM generated assignment orders for our Marines to go overseas (OCONUS) or return to the Contiguous United States (CONUS). It was an assignment model helping us optimize which Marines to assign to their next duty station. Today, we might refer to EAM modules as Human Capital Management (HCM) or a Human Resource Information System (HRIS).

Before the late 1980s, we had been processing reserve and active-duty Marines in two separate systems, and we started looking for a way to combine the two human resource management processes into one consolidated system. One drawback of the old system, for example, occurred when generating assignments. If we had a Marine reservist serving their community as a Police Officer, but he or she was a Mechanic on active duty, which Military Occupational Specialty (MOS) should we prioritize in our algorithms for upcoming mission sets? The combined system gave us an efficient way to assess both occupations.

For me, these were exciting active-duty tours, and the software technologies I learned opened up avenues in computer science that, in college, I did not even know existed. Then after my active duty tours ended, I became a Reservist and returned to Quantico, VA where I was an Instructor at the Computer Sciences School (CSS). After CSS, I was assigned to support an Opposing Force (OPFOR) team at the Armed Forces Staff College in Norfolk, VA. We were involved in simulated war-gaming exercises—another dynamic and innovative use of data, systems, and computer science.

My First Experiences with Computers

Looking back, my first contact with a "computer" was in high school. We had an old UPI teletype machine connected via modem with its own paper on a roll where one could type or select from its keyboard anything about careers. It would print what data it had available about any selected career.

Next, I worked with computers at Temple University. My original major was architecture, but in hindsight, I am so very glad we were required to take computer science classes. Discovering how computers actually worked changed my life, and the "Wow!" of it all sold me on computers as a career. I was thrilled when I commanded the computer to act in specific ways when I entered specific codes.

Computers had become ultra-fascinating, and architecture had become time consuming and tortuous. So, changing my major from architecture to computer science had become a "no brainer."

How and When I Heard About BDPA

On campus at Temple, we heard a radio commercial that went something like this: "If you want to know anything about computers, but are afraid to ask, come on down to Girard Bank and find out more about computers and data processing with the Black Data Processing Associates." That was in 1983, and that's how I first heard about BDPA. I attended the meeting, then the late Juan Noyles and I started a student BDPA Chapter at Temple University.

Transitioning from Active Duty

What I've described, thus far, are the first several years of my 16-year military career. After I separated from active duty, I remained in the reserves and started my fulltime civilian career with Perot Systems Corporation, in Washington, D.C. where I followed up with Margaret "Midge" Johnson. She was already working at Perot Systems and referred me to their MCI Commercial Billing team. In 1990, also in Washington, D.C., I had the pleasure to serve as Chairman of BDPA's National Technology Conference where both MCI and Perot Systems were major conference sponsors.

During the last 30 years, I was an MIS Director for two trade associations (ITAA and ITSA); helped launch an HBCU Project Office (HPO); provided contractor support to a $27 million DoD Mentor-Protégé

Program (MPP); directed business intelligent transportation systems (ITS), defense (DoD), and Intelligence Community (IC) engagements. These efforts helped small business teams win Federal Highway Administration (FHWA), Small Business, and DoD Nunn-Perry awards.

My Message to BDPA Audiences

If I were speaking at a BDPA Program Meeting or Meet-Up—whether in 1983 or today—my message would be the same: "Build your professional network. Continue to build and nurture these networks, and always have trade associations as an integral part of your resume and professional growth." Let people in your trade know that you respect the trade, have an interest in that trade, and are dedicated to honing required skillsets. Moreover, your affiliation with organizations like ACM, AFCEA, and BDPA highlight your technical skills, teamwork and accomplishments. When hiring managers see this on your resume, they say to themselves, "Hey, this person wants more than just a job; they are genuinely interested in the type of work we do here."

I+Plus Magazine

As mentioned earlier, I've produced magazines since third grade. And my lifelong interest in publishing was instrumental in the launch of *I+Plus* magazine. BDPA members who were active back in 1991, might remember that launch. The Magazine's tagline was, *"An Information Systems Magazine for Tomorrow's Workforce."*

One of my mentors, at the time, was the late Ollie Morgan of the Chicago BDPA Chapter. Ollie and I talked all the time, and I was impressed with his accomplishments; he had three newsletters rolling off the presses at the same time. To me, Ollie was a rock star, and absolutely without question, Ollie was a "mover and a shaker" who made things happen. And for a while in BDPA, Ollie Morgan seemed leaps and bounds above the rest of BDPA in terms of corporate advisory councils (CACs), advertising ideas, sponsorship acquisition, revenue generation, and a futuristic vision for what a magazine representing an organization like BDPA ought to be. Ollie held my undivided attention. And anything you hear about "*I+Plus Magazine*," or "*bdpatoday*," all props should go to Ollie Morgan.

Ollie knew that organizations must "publish or perish," because publishing—getting the word out about who we are and what we do—is almost as important as who we are and what we do. For example, if BDPA had not advertised on WDAS radio back in 1983, I might never have heard about BDPA.

The design of *I+Plus Magazine* focused on the academic and tech-professional aspects of "publish or perish." Because BDPA has a large reservoir of talent and expertise in academia and industry, *I+Plus*

Magazine was intended to capture white papers and opinions from information technology, computer science, supercomputing, quantum technology, and cyber professionals; our colleagues who are creating and teaching. We wanted them to write articles in a BDPA quarterly magazine which would be our industry's professional magazine. That is what *I+Plus* Magazine was designed to do; to try to be the "Black Enterprise Magazine" for the information technology and communication technology industries, published by BDPA.

bdpatoday Publications

We created *"bdpatoday"* to promote the 2007 National Conference which the D.C. Chapter was hosting. The conference was in August, and it was already May, which meant we had to "publish" something about the Conference before Howard University's graduation occurring in a week, or our hopes of attracting a throng of attendees to our Conference, would literally "perish."So here we were in May, and absolutely nothing had had come out of any of our communications teams. So, I picked up the phone and asked, "Is there anything you've published about our Conference? It's May, and Howard graduates next week." We already knew the answer was "No." Therefore in 2007, we launched *bdpatoday*, and over the years, *bdpatoday* has transformed from a print magazine to a modern social media platform.

bdpatoday Magazine Cover

This weekend we will reach fifteen thousand followers on LinkedIn. We have a Facebook presence, an Instagram presence, and we have *bdpatoday* on YouTube, which is an integral part of our YouTube

Popular Technology TV (PTTV) social media platform.

The *bdpatoday* social media platform was designed for local chapters to use, so that each chapter can configure its own flavor of *bdpatoday*. I'd like to continue conversations with our national board and officers about making this happen. Then from there, BDPA might begin building comprehensive marketing, talent and opportunity development platforms, leveraging what we learned building the *bdpatoday* social media platform.

In the last two years we have been working with the Black Press USA, the National Newspaper Publishers Association; Dr. Benjamin Chavis. The intent right now is to continue our work with Congress, state, and local legislators to actually fund technology publications in Black newspapers, Black and Brown newspapers, and the Black, Indigenous, and People of Color (BIPOC) community. In essence, we would have at least one *bdpatoday* publication every month because our proposal covers STEM. Readers would have a print or digital magazine, very similar to "*Parade Magazine*" in our Sunday papers, as an insert. Monthly STEM topics would rotate, so week one would be Science editions; week two would be the Technology [*bdpatoday*] edition; week three would be the Engineering edition; followed by the Mathematics edition in week four.

Every four weeks, readers would have a different publication in each of our BIPOC newspapers in America, both print and digital. This effort creates new jobs that deliver content and helps bridge digital divides. We can help narrow, close, or mitigate "news deserts," because when we look hard at our big picture, mainstream media and Black media simply are not covering technology the way our community needs them to do with us and for us. That is our new multimedia role and our vision for *bdpatoday*. Shoutout to BDPA National President Mr. Terry Morris. He and his team created the hashtag #BDPAfuture.

Oracle Scholars and Navy ROTC

Over the years, my U.S. military connections have helped BDPA. Leading up to the 2009 BDPA technology conference in Raleigh, North Carolina, I asked Charles Phillips, President of Oracle, to be our keynote speaker. Charles and I were cadets at the United States Air Force Academy, and we both ended up serving our nation as Marine Corps Officers. Although Charles was not able to keynote, Oracle awarded $50,000 to National BDPA, and BDPA has maintained a student scholarship program with Oracle ever since.

More good fortune was on the way because Acting Secretary of the Navy, the Honorable B.J. Penn, stepped in as our keynote speaker, and at that same 2009 conference, the United States Navy presented its first full NROTC Scholarship to one of our High School Computer Competition (HSCC) students, Ms. Lisa "Raven" Stevenson, from the Greater Columbia

Chapter of BDPA. Upon graduation from Duke University in 2013, Ms. Stevenson was commissioned an Ensign in the United States Navy.

In 2020 and 2021, the U.S. Air Force co-hosted their annual AFRL STTR HBCU/MSI Outreach Initiative Collider with National BDPA's annual technology conference. This was a unique opportunity to bring small businesses, HBCUs, and BDPA tech industry mission partners together "under one roof" to collaborate and innovate.

The Grant

The Washington, D.C. chapter won a $300,000 grant from Microsoft in 2020. BDPA's mission partners, Mr. Raymond Bell, Jr., with the H.O.P.E. Project DMV in Washington, D.C., partnered with BDPA-DC in the proposal to Microsoft.

This grant enables BDPA and HOPE to offer workforce upskilling development and technical skills training with mentoring. Microsoft and CompTIA certification training is also provided. High school students, some of whom are "High School Computer Competition" (HSCC) students, and a few college student members serve as Interns. We are working with some of the largest technology companies in the world. Now, we are moving all of our content slowly but surely into augmented-reality and virtual-reality worlds. Imagine this—access to an African-American technology museum wherever we are, or wherever we need to be.

Our interns are starting out with BDPA history. If one were to actually visit our Pinterest site (pinterest.com/bdpatoday), we have several boards with over 4000 pins. There is a lot of Black History, BDPA history, technology history, video clips, and also recent publications of *bdpatoday*, both monthly and our weekly *In Case You Missed "I.T."* (ICYMI) editions.

We are handing off these subtasks to our interns and tech students to make BDPA content available in virtual-reality or augmented-reality platforms. As industry changes, our content will actually change with it.

Our *Tablets for Teens* program was launched in 2017 to provide BDPA Student Members, BDPA Interns, JROTC Cadets, or high school students enrolled in BDPA's Student I.T. Education and Scholarships (SITES) programs opportunities to receive new tablets or notebook PCs from BDPA sponsors. BDPA SITES students from Chapters in Baton Rouge, Detroit, Huntsville, Philadelphia and Washington, D.C. have received new notebook PCs and tablets from HP and Samsung with services from AT&T and T-Mobile.

BDPA's 50th Anniversary in 2025

In our Nation's Capital, the Biden Administration is putting together a multi-trillion dollar infrastructure package. We have positioned BDPA chapters to participate, and we are also working with staffers on input for the 2022 National Defense Authorization Act (NDAA). Washington, D.C. is unique because we also are co-located with the federal government and Congress.

One area our community must improve is how we work with Congress to secure TECH2025 funding and appropriations for all of BDPA's U.S. SITES programs. Moreover, we need to improve how we pursue local BDPA Chapter Community Project Funding (CPF) requests through FY25. In Washington, D.C., we are preparing for National BDPA's fiftieth anniversary in 2025, and we hope to be one of the cities that hosts major events. Ideally, BDPA chapters in every state will participate.

BDPA Chapters outside of our Nation's Capital have to make sure that all state senators, county, and local government officials know about BDPA and its track record of success. Moreover, BDPA chapter cities like Cleveland, Philadelphia, Boston, New York, Atlanta, Minneapolis, St. Louis, and Dallas are co-located with Federal Reserve districts that have budgets supporting community organizations and events.

Building Tomorrow Today

From a banking technology or FinTech perspective, cryptocurrency is on track to revolutionize commerce for several decades. Therefore, if we have connections with people already involved in FinTech, then we can help people in our communities obtain the resulting job and business opportunities that undoubtedly will emerge. And to position ourselves to be ready to capitalize on these opportunities, BDPA should invite bank representatives to continue working with BDPA.

As previously mentioned, we are entrusting responsibility to our interns and our young students to make BDPA content available for streaming in virtual-reality and augmented-reality "infotainment" worlds. And as industry changes, that content will actually change with it, because the excitement about BDPA continues to be about the unlimited potential of our future.

Dr. Ademola O. Solaru

CHAPTER 13

Dr. Ademola O. Solaru

Dr. Ademola O. Solaru (Demo) is a tech entrepreneur who is the architect of several online health-services platforms, including the ProviderGateway and the Grandwire platforms which link organizations and Providers in Health and Human Services delivery networks. Born in Lagos, Nigeria, Demo is a long-time BDPA member, and he is Co-Founder of the BDPA IT-Corps. In a January 23, 2021 interview, Demo talked about life, his career, and BDPA.

Build Beyond Borders—The IT Corps

By Dr. Ademola O. Solaru

I came here from Nigeria in 1975, or thereabouts, to go to school at Purdue University in West Lafayette, Indiana. I was a computer science major at a time when, unlike now, many of us were just hoping to become software programmers. In Nigeria, in Africa, computer science was something I saw from far away because in 1975, computers were not commonplace anywhere, let alone there. But I came here to Purdue University, and over a period of time, I got my undergraduate degree, went to graduate school at Eastern Michigan, and finally got a Doctorate in Management from Case Western Reserve University—all with a focus on the management of technology.

While I was in graduate school, I worked at a small software firm that gave me the first inspiration of what I thought I would like to do in life. We were selling and installing what was then called a mini-computer. And I was one of those guys who wrote software and went to our various locations to install the software on them. There was no internet to install software remotely, so we had to drive around town to physically install the software. But it was a great place; it was a tiny company; it was like four or five people; and it was wonderful.

And later on, I went to work for a consulting firm, a small consulting firm, and that took me to Ford Motor Company at the world headquarters, in Detroit. I did one brief stint there, and I did another brief stint at General Motors. So I had an opportunity to see what the big corporate life was like. And in a way, that really wasn't my thing; the corporate life; it wasn't really for me. But at that time when I was just getting my feet wet, I didn't know that there was going to be any other way. That was just the way it worked, back then. The corporations were the people who had the computers. There were no personal computers (PCs) to speak of. The PC wasn't born yet.

Ernst and Young

And then I went to work for a Big-8 accounting firm, which was Ernst and Young. It wasn't called Ernst & Young yet; it was Ernst & Whinney, and it merged with Arthur Young a little while later to become Ernst & Young. I worked in the multinationals part of the organization, so I worked in Nigeria for a bit. And then I came to Cleveland to work, where the focus of my early going was just getting reporting up into the database systems of the multinationals. And it was helpful that I'd had big-corporate experience with Ford and General Motors. So I understood how this might work, and so forth.

Laventhol & Horvath

And then later on, at some point, I worked for Laventhol & Horvath, which was also an accounting firm.

And practically all these accounting firms were working for companies that had branches everywhere. So there was a lot of opportunity for either auditing systems, reporting on systems, or making recommendations for systems. It was a lot more than just coding software programs, even though, eventually, I did get my hands wet by the time the IBM PC came along with converting certain mainframe systems to be on PCs.

So I enjoyed all of those experiences, and that kind of framed where I am today, because the background was taking big-time systems, putting them on a PC, and also being able to walk around a lot of people's organizations. I was never just stuck in a cubicle. I flew everywhere, went everywhere, spoke to management, spoke to people in the trenches, and interacted with people in manufacturing.

On a project we did with the Indiana Toll Road—while I was with Laventhol & Horvath—I was actually in a ticket booth giving tickets to people going through the tunnel just to know how exactly the system worked. You might think that's overkill, but that was just one of those experiences that shaped me.

Mid-America Consulting Group

Then I met with a gentleman in Cleveland who owned Mid-America Consulting Group, and we became partners in Mid-America Consulting Group; a small consulting firm was what I was seeking, and we did that very successfully, I would say, one of the few successful partnerships, because that lasted about 25 years. And we eventually split up, very, very amicably. And everybody went their separate ways because we had developed three or four partners who wanted to do different things. And I started Parthenon GlobalSystems in 2009, and eventually split with Mid-America Consulting Group in 2016. And the rest, as they say, is history.

Parthenon GlobalSystems

Parthenon GlobalSystems has a product that I am actually very proud of because I birthed that product in 1998. So you can imagine the number of product-feature improvements it's been through in 22 years. And in those 22 years, it has stood the test of time. It's gone through maybe six or seven iterations under the same product name. It's been different things at different times, but now it is the backbone of prior authorization in Medicaid for nursing facilities throughout the state of Ohio, and for contract management in the state of Wisconsin also. So that's sort of the prime area that I finally landed in. And all of my prior experiences, and education, and lessons learned, and bumps and bruises have prepared me for where I am today at Parthenon GlobalSystems.

Black Data Processing Associates

And it was during that journey that Ken Wilson, who also happens to be my brother-in-law, invited me to come to a BDPA meeting. I don't know if he mandated me to come to a meeting or invited me, but either way, that had to happen. And it was at that first meeting that I met the very charismatic Norman Mays who was leading that meeting at the time. And I got to find out that he was actually the founder of the chapter. So it was a wonderful beginning. I think there were 45, 50 people at the first meeting I came to. So it was a wonderful meeting to have come to, and so that's sort of how I started with BDPA.

In BDPA, the first thing that was satisfying for me was that there were all these black people around technology with the same concerns, not just for ourselves, but for the next generation coming into it; everybody with a can-do spirit; everybody also caught up in the vortex of technology development, at that time, that basically sucked you into the movement; that you've got to be doing something in technology; that you've got to be learning a new language, or building a new product, or learning what's possible with PCs. It was a very exciting time in technology because whether servers were going to be the future, whether mainframes were going to survive, whether PCs could be taken seriously, we were at the cusp of brand new products. We were there at the very beginning. There was no Google yet. There was no Internet yet, so that everything was possible. Everything was possible.

So when I got involved with BDPA and started talking to both Ken, who had a company at the time that was pretty novel for its time; the fact that he had all of these contracts; all of these people working for him. And I eventually worked for Ken.

And then speaking to Norman, who also had the big corporate experience and big military experience, and so forth, I took them seriously when basically looking for various challenges. How do we address this? How do we address that? And it was just wide open, and that was very good to say.

Well, let me interject myself into this narrative. One of my big concerns during that time was: Because we were Black Data Processing Associates and trying to find our way into technology, there was a lot of asking. We were asking the big corporates how we plug in because they were the big employers. So there's no point in just being excited about technology if you never work anywhere. That was good. And Ken, for example, was an example of somebody who took the bull by the horns already and found his way into the corporate as a contractor, and as an employer himself, and that was quite an inspiration that it even happened. I mean, in the late 70s and early 80s, that was scary, impressive, actually.

So in speaking about what should we do: We're not asking now. We are bringing something to the table that is going to be of value, that is going to be valued by our own community and by the broader community. How should we frame who we are? We're not knocking on your door to ask for a favor or ask to be let in or to be included. All of those things are necessary. But we are now at this point where we're saying that we are noticing we have a lot of talent, a lot of people who know what they're doing. They put the time in. How should we do this *IT Corps* thing?

BDPA IT Corps

So we were still talking about it, and Norman said, "Well, we've got to think as big and as boldly as possible. This should be a global phenomenon." Somehow we got from just Cleveland to national to global, and one thing led to another. We talked about, "Well, there is this conference by Leon Sullivan that actually goes all the way to Africa," and so forth. And this is the part of my own heart strings that were being pulled, saying that it's not just here; it's everywhere we've got this issue. So one way or the other, we went on this excursion to Tanzania, Africa that was sponsored by BDPA. And I'm very grateful for that experience.

And we went there, and it was like a ground floor opportunity to go and talk to the powerbrokers. And we even strayed away from the conference: We went into the rural area, to a school, addressed the school, and they corresponded with us for quite some time after we departed. And when we got back from the trip, it was like, well, you know what? We got to a point I looked Ken in the eye, I looked Norman in the eye, and it was like, "Yeah, I get it, it's showtime." What are we going to do? And that led to the formation of the *IT Corps*. And the *IT Corps* name was even deliberate to say, look, if you're going to do something global, be careful that you don't exclude anyone inadvertently just because it's the Black Data Processing Associates. So many people are drawn to BDPA that we kept BDPA in the name, but the *IT Corps* was explained as something that's like a Peace Corps. You're going to solve a real-world problem. And that, for me, always did it. The feeling that I'm producing value: My input is valued, my expertise is valued, and I have something to prove. That's personal for me.

In the first instance, it's part of why it was difficult for me to be in the corporate world, because in certain situations you're just one of thousands. And so it really jelled for me, mentoring the young people we have; we're already doing that. But this was spectacular because we found out, very early, that we have many, many geniuses among our young people, if we would just ask them, and value them, and believe they have something to offer to begin with.

So the mentoring, it was almost like they were mentoring us on how to engage young people. And so we just said, alright, we'll just lay a few problems down, and see what they come up with, and don't try to tell them. Don't try to teach them what to say or how to come about it. And that was one of the most spectacular summers that we had; the initiation of the *IT Corps*.

And so the kids came together. I recall it was supposed to be a six week program initially. And by the time we were done, the kids refused to end the program in the summer and stayed with us for like four months apiece just with continuous input, guidance on what they were doing, and feedback and things like that.

So that was proof that we were right about engaging this way; not telling kids, "You can be whatever you want to be." That is necessary. That is absolutely necessary. But also giving that room to say, alright, I have a problem: It's a societal problem; It's a spiritual problem: It's a community problem; It's a problem of access; It's all kinds of things. We had brought some community leaders together from Cleveland Clinic; I recall a physician from Cleveland Clinic. We brought a cleric; a priest from a local church. We had brought someone who ran the largest nonprofit organization in Cleveland; the Gund Foundation.

And we said, no, we are not here to talk about technology. Just tell us what's going on in our society and in our community. And we're going to take these problems; we don't want to solve them ourselves; we want to give it to our kids and ask them the question that says, "With these problems that we have, how would you apply technology to solving?" And I think that should be the way BDPA actually functions today. We're not a ground floor company any longer. People have been in technology 20, 30, 40 years. We're not trying to get in. We are trying to say, "We have something to offer." Many more people are engaged with technology now. Many more people have laptops and apps. It's not like it used to be. So I think the *IT Corps* can, if you will, can modify the DNA of BDPA to say we have something to offer, and we are not asking to be included. There are so many problems out here that obviously don't have a solution. We should be attacking it that way. So that's kind of how I wound up with the IT Corps, and what it still means to me today.

I Became President

My time as Cleveland Chapter President was actually a major learning opportunity for me personally. My presidential adventure began in 2010. The Internet had come about, and we had a meeting every month at John Carroll University, but we were having quite a challenge with people coming to meetings, and a lot of people had moved on. It was reflective of our own core networks. People had retired, people were working overtime, people were moving out of state. Mostly their job had taken them out of that locus, that comfort area that made it easy for people to want to come to the meetings. And we were so focused and insistent on our old way of doing things. And Wayne Hicks was the one who said, "Well, look, listen, guys, let's take a good, hard look at the way you're doing this. You need to call the public to come to these meetings and make them very, very interesting. Don't make it a membership drive or anything. Focus on something that people want to know. And lo and behold, we went with the "MeetUp" platform, and our program meetings went from four or five people to 30, 35 people, just like that. And we even started to challenge ourselves about how should we present our programs. It got even more compelling when we had pizza; when we had something to eat. I made, I recall, about fourteen or sixteen different presentations that I still have the recordings of that have to do with big data, which was a big draw because people were very, very interested in big data, smart cities, what was happening in medicine, even the legal implications of the Internet, like Net Neutrality, and so forth.

Economic Opportunities in the Cloud

Around the time of the 2008-2009 recession, before we even got to the years we were doing the MeetUps, there was the recession uncertainty of, "What fate or fortune does our future hold." And around that time, we started talking about "cloud computing," and that conversation began with "What exactly is cloud computing?" Then we moved very quickly to, "What is the commercial implication of cloud computing, and what are the implications for us?" And I will say that these types of conversations amongst members are one of the benefits of belonging to BDPA. And in my own company, we started thinking, "Wait a minute: Why exactly do we still have inhouse data centers?" Let's get involved with this, and do something productive with this cloud computing opportunity. So we eventually started reengineering our company to become a cloud-based company.

But, the point I'm trying to underscore is this: When we get together as BDPA, and we ask ourselves: What is our purpose for getting together? Why don't we just join any old tech organization? And what's so special about being in a Black Data Processing Associates that's got an identification with African-Americans in particular? Well, the answer to all three of these questions is **economic opportunity,** because economic opportunity for African-Americans in technology jobs was nonexistent before BDPA was born in 1975.

But cloud computing now gives us fighting chance. For example: Any time you can do something along the lines of catalog sales that people are just buying pure value. They don't care who's behind the catalog. So create a catalog then.

The same thing is happening in cloud computing. Put a solution in the cloud. It levels the playing field instantly because now people judge by either you now have value to offer, or you don't. And many of the old obstacles are out of the way. And it's very important for BDPA to know to concentrate on that.

When we get together at BDPA in meetings, it is the economic and empowerment opportunity presented through technology that is of interest—that is of paramount importance. And that economic and empowerment opportunity can take us where we want to go.

It's very liberating to say: If you were to conquer the earth, and you were king for a day, and you were the emperor of the world for a day, how would you use technology to actually rein in this empowerment for yourself, for your community, for the group that you're with, or for whatever your interests are?

So I would always address a group, whether it was back in the eighties when I came around, or even now, to say: Don't get together and talk about how we don't do this, or how we don't do that, or there's a smart brother over here, or a smart sister over there who's just been made the Secretary of Commerce, or this and that. And it's good because in their achievement, there is access. But that is just one data point. How can we be part of that data point and say: This is how I would harness the technology infrastructure that is present? So in the 70s or 80s, it was publish some software, and sell it, and see how far you get. Put it on a PC. That was a burgeoning opportunity back then; publish something. The Internet has made it possible to publish apps. So basically, put it out there.

Now, as far as speaking to entrepreneurs today about where I see things going, there is something that is happening already, that you see all around you; and that "something" is the **business of platforms**. And platforms come in two flavors; **platform as technology** versus **platform as a business**. They are distinct, and it is very easy to confuse the two because we are used to using the word platform ambiguously.

As soon as we see the word platform, many of us who have been in the business, even those who haven't, think in terms of some kind of technology platform, or some series of technologies.

But "platform as a business" is different. It is related, but it just basically says, take Amazon for example. Amazon is a platform business. There are multiple creators of value and there are multiple consumers of value. And Amazon gets benefits coming and going. Apple, the phone, is also a platform. There are multiple creators (developers) of Apple apps, and there are multiple consumers (users) of Apple apps. This multi-sidedness of a platform (the creators side, and the consumers side) is the business concept to build and concentrate on. That is to say: Always build something where there will be multiple creators of value, and multiple consumers of value. What we have been used to, is building something where there's one creator of value, and one consumer of value.

So, if I do a tenant-property management system, there is only one type of creator of value—a property manager. And there is only one type of consumer that can come to me—a tenant. Amazon started that way. They were just trying to sell books, but look at where they are today. Everything that they have done, they have tried to figure out how many different types of creators of value (producers) can there be on this platform, and how many types of consumers. This means that in platform businesses, every expertise you have relating to technology is valuable. So, for example, I'm starting ABC Pet Grooming, and I needed to set up my accounting interest structure. So I got a recommendation on using this economic package, and I went to their platform, and of course I wasn't thinking platform at all. All I was trying to do was buy the accounting package, and of course, in the back of my head I'm thinking, all right, to set this thing up, I'm going to have to know my chart of accounts and all that stuff. And setting this stuff up is tedious, time consuming, and not fun.

But on their website, they also have the names by geographical area of people who could help me set it up. So, it's very important to understand that this ecosystem of "setting it up" this way was a deliberate business strategy by the platform owners. So I thought, OK, well, I click on this; I bought the product. I clicked on that; I found the guy. And then this person calls me, and he says, "Oh! Since you have accounting, how are you going to do your payroll?" I said, "I'm not sure." And he says, "Then click on that payroll product over there," not made by the same company, but it contains the needed value. "Well, we also need..." It became we also need a bill payment system. And he says, "Well, I have access to this bill payment system, and it interacts with your accounting and payroll systems." So all of a sudden, a complex accounting system, including an accountant, came together quickly. Yet I only started with one company, and that is deliberate. So they have partners that say, "I can create the core value you're looking for, which is an accounting system. I don't do payroll, but I can get a partner who can bring that. I don't provide advice, but I can give you a network of people around the country who do this."

So we have to think in those terms. Think about what I'm saying. Now, imagine that one BDPA person creates a platform, and let's say it's in plumbing, or anything, and says, "Oh, look, I need someone who knows about implementing this device, and I want to feature them on my platform," and we interact that way. And there are kids who are creating apps, and "You know what? I could use that app." Some apps are even more benign in the interface, such as a calculator or something, or estimator that doesn't interface with anything, but it says people are looking for value.

You go to Amazon, it doesn't matter what you're looking for, you just believe it's there. And any time you search for something, you search enough for something, and Amazon says they have searched 15 times for the "Nose LaBarge" system. They go and get one because they know it's in demand. And we have to think not about building everything, but about being in the business of building platforms, because consumers want to be satisfied in one place. It's like going to the mall, that kind of thing.

So going forward, that's what I advise right now, and that's where I see the big opportunity going forward, as you can see from Facebook and Twitter. And those are the big ones, the big and obvious examples, but it is saying that this business model is becoming the actual frontier that we have to pay attention to going forward.

We've Got to Do Something—More

So, what BDPA could do that would really excite me now is actually along the lines of platform saying, we have 55 chapters, and we celebrate what this chapter is doing versus what that chapter is doing, and so on and so forth, harnessing and bringing all those together as value means when something happens in the St. Louis chapter, or something happens in the Detroit chapter, we should find a way to be able to be able to publish it, and harness that benefit for another group.

So, competing with each other is great because, you know, we've got all these competitions and contests among the young people, but cooperating and aligning with each other is even greater. That's even greater. That's where the power actually lies.

There's a place where there is talk. And then there's action. That's exactly what happened with IT Corps. There was talk until the point where it was like, "Okay, we're going to keep talking about it or we're going to do something." And then all of a sudden you find that, hey, Cleveland, Detroit and St. Louis are interested in this idea. That's good enough. You don't have to wait for everybody. You get your kids to write apps that do XYZ. I'll do ABC, and the other chapter will do PQR. And here's how they're going to interact. And in the first year it's going to look kludgy, but the second year it's going to create value. And let's see whether this is something, you know, even taking for some of the IT Corps things that we talked about, where we spoke to the Cleveland Clinic. And one of the issues that they have in our communities are people winding up in the emergency room because they have poor, or no, healthcare insurance. But there is real, negative financial impact to the society when that happens to them personally, to the community, and to the health care organization that has to absorb the cost when they show up in the emergency room. So imagine this, that on our platform, we have a place where you can get a Fitbit, that you have someone who can talk you through monitoring your vitals through this Fitbit, that we have someone who provides a communications app access so that you can upload the data. It can be done automatically, that we have someone and maybe someone in Cincinnati who says, yeah, as soon as that data comes in about you, we are good at analyzing this and we can create individual dashboards for people. And then someone else provides consultation about the implications of this or that, and someone else knows the healthcare providers in your area that you see anytime the dashboard red light trips, which is going to initiate something else, and so forth. All kinds of things start to happen when we actually start to do it. Otherwise, it's great that you said it before, and we can talk about it forever, or we could do something because I think our forums in BDPA need to produce something. Yeah, it's great to talk about it, but we have to produce something.

Terry Morris

CHAPTER 14

Terry Morris

Terry Morris, the National President of the Black Data Processing Associates (BDPA) organization in 2021, is "Advisor, Racial Justice," for Eli Lilly and Company, where he has worked for more than 20 years. Terry has served in several leadership roles at Eli Lilly, including "Director of Global Services Solutions," in the Information and Digital Solutions division. Terry earned a Bachelor of Science degree in Computer and Information Systems at Florida A&M University, and a Master of Policy Analysis at Indiana-Purdue University. He is a community servant, activist, and member, director, and/or chairman of several prominent non-profit boards of directors. And in 2018, Terry was named to be named one of Indianapolis' "40 under

40," by the Indianapolis Business Journal. In a February 5, 2021 interview, Terry talked about life, his career, and BDPA. These conversations are shared below.

Help People Move Mountains

By Terry Morris

I grew up in a little town called Perry Florida, so you can call me Terry from Perry. Back then, Perry had a population of seven thousand people. So it's one of those towns where "everybody knows everybody," or they, at least, know somebody who knows you or your parents. You're always being watched by somebody in a community like that, so you learn, early on, to think twice about what you do.

I was the second child born to a mom who was 15 years old, so I ended up being raised by my grandparents; my dad's parents. And they made sure we had all of the necessities of life, not necessarily all of the extras, but the necessities were always there. And we counted ourselves blessed for that.

When I got to the seventh grade, my English teacher saw some potential in me. She was the consummate Florida A&M Rattler (FAMU). And when she heard me mention a college that was not her beloved FAMU, she began correcting my course by asking my grandparents if she could take me to Florida A&M football games. And every time she went to a game, I was in the back seat with her son going to a game as well. So that's how I ended up at Florida A&M University.

Now, my career path to information technology (IT) was a little different. I was working at a Little Caesars Pizza shop in Perry, and had saved five hundred dollars to buy a computer. So, when I went to the only computer shop in Perry, and happened to run into the owner, and shared with him my desire to buy a $500 computer, he politely informed me that $500 was way below what it cost to buy a computer, in 1994. But as luck would have it, he called me up later, and asked, "How about I offer you a job?" And I took that job he offered me. And as a sophomore in high school, I was creating web pages. And back in 1994, web pages were just becoming a thing. So that job—at GulfNet Consulting—launched me on a tech-career trajectory that continued in college.

At Florida A&M, I majored in Computer and Information Systems, and I joined the Association for Computing Machinery (ACM), eventually becoming Chapter President of that non-profit tech association. In ACM, I had the opportunity to participate in and learn to appreciate the value of initiatives that benefited and supported communities of people focused on computing.

And it was as a sophomore in college, that I attended a career-planning conference sponsored by Eli Lilly & Company (Lilly). It was 1998—the first year of that conference—and in that conference, they would invite students from Historically Black Colleges and

Universities (HBCUs), to come to Indianapolis and experience a little bit of Lilly's corporate culture. And at the time Lilly's tagline was, "Answers that Matter." And Lilly's slogan, "Answers that Matter", and its corporate culture won the day for me. And I must have impressed them too because they offered me an internship.

However, I had a previous commitment, working for the FAMU Institute for Urban Policy, and they had just won a grant from Governor Jeb Bush to help close the "digital divide" in and around the State of Florida. I was asked to run that grant program that provided me an opportunity to travel throughout the State of Florida and help underrepresented communities "close the digital divide." It was an opportunity I simply could not pass up. So I chose to do that work in lieu of accepting the Lilly internship.

After graduation, I did accept an opportunity at Lilly, and I've worked at Lilly for more than twenty years, in various information technology (IT) units. My most recent IT job involved serving as Director of Global Services Solutions where I was responsible for delivering digital solutions to HR, Legal, Ethics, Compliance, and other departments. Additionally, I was involved with helping Lilly identify and attract talented business-technology professionals.

But it was late last year that I decided to move into Lilly's Global Diversity organization. In my current position, I serve as "Advisor, Racial Justice," working on a team advancing Lilly's efforts to build and maintain an equitable work environment inside our corporate walls and beyond.

Back in 2009, I was invited, through Lilly sponsorship, to attend my first BDPA National Conference. At the time, I had no idea who this BDPA was. But attending the 2009 National Conference in Raleigh, North Carolina changed my life in wonderful ways. Meeting black leaders from across the US and around the world who were improving people's lives opened my eyes and lifted my personal and professional aspirations of what was possible. So I joined, and started actively engaging with other members of the BDPA Indianapolis Chapter.My participation in BDPA continually intensified, and in 2014, I became Chapter President. Ultimately, my work in BDPA was just beginning, and I continued serving the Indianapolis Chapter as President until 2017, when I ran for, and was elected, National President of BDPA, which is where I am today, and why we're having this conversation.

Why I Pursued Leadership in BDPA

Faith is a big part of my tradition. And there's a scripture that says, To whom much is given, much is required." And I've mentioned some examples of where I've been given a whole bunch. And because of my faith, my upbringing, and because of the abundance of blessings that have been bestowed upon me, I am not surprised by the fact that a desire to give back has become a fundamental part of who I am.

As with many of us, there were seasons in my life when I stumbled, and my trajectory was flat or downward. But I was always able to—with the help of somebody giving back to me—hit the reset button, and point my life trajectory back upward. And those experiences deepened my commitment to making a positive difference in someone else's life, particularly in the lives of people in underrepresented communities, because we don't always get the same resources that are typically available to people who are more well-off.

◆

Equity—equal opportunity. That's what's missing, and that's why organizations like BDPA are devoted to chipping away at the glass ceilings and barriers to success that are blocking our progress. And in BDPA, I saw an opportunity to join a team of people who were already chipping away at these barriers.

So, I was shocked to not have known about BDPA prior to 2009. Because BDPA had been doing what it was doing for decades—helping students, helping IT professionals, and helping communities. And as I got closer to the center of BDPA, I started hearing that "BDPA is one of the world's best kept secrets." But the way I see it, BDPA should not be a secret. And one of my main motivations for wanting to lead the Indianapolis Chapter, and the National organization, is my desire to divulge that secret, and get the word out to the world that BDPA helps students, helps IT professionals, and helps communities.

So, I count myself blessed to be able to support this organization that has been helping people for more than 46 years. It is phenomenal doing the work that we're doing in the season that we are doing it. We have challenges, but we've built a financially solvent organization, we've built a solid base, and we're building a strong reserve.

There's never been a more important time to be exceptional.

There is a book called "The Four" by Scott Galloway that explores the societal impacts of four technology giants; Apple, Amazon, Facebook, and Google. And in that book, there's a chapter called "The T Algorithm," where the "T" stands for "Trillion," because each of the four tech behemoths are worth more than one trillion dollars. And Amazon, alone, is worth more than Walmart, Target, Kroger, Nordstrom, Tiffany & Co., Coach, Williams-Sonoma, Tesco, Ikea, Carrefour, and The Gap combined. Tech has taken over. So for BDPA, the trillion-dollar "T" should also stand for "Tech," because tech opportunity—today and in the foreseeable future—is a clear and present pathway to a brighter future for our members, for our students, and for our communities. And there's a quote that really resonated with me where it says, "There's never been a more important time to be exceptional, or a worse time to be average." And that is the message that our team is conveying to our membership; to lean into the energy that is available to us, in spite of the fact that racial inequities continue to plague our people. We've all experienced them in many respects. But the tech window of opportunity to a brighter future is where I am calling for our folks to bring the very best of who we are to the forefront. And we, in BDPA, want to support that.

BDPA Tech Talks

For example, we host a "Tech Talk" technology series that happens monthly, live online. In each "Tech Talk" episode, we host an expert from a business-tech organization who shares stories and experiences about how they successfully led business-tech organizations and initiatives. We bring in guests from our member's organizations, from organizations like the big four (Apple, Amazon, Facebook, and Google), and from many, many more.

Historically Black Colleges and Universities (HBCUs)

Also, we are reawakening our college footprint. In the past, BDPA has organized college chapters. And in the current evolutionary iteration of BDPA, we're bringing that back. We've already restarted a college chapter at Florida A&M University, Purdue, and Virginia State University. And we're talking with Morehouse and Hampton Universities. I was on a phone call yesterday with Texas Southern University, with their Dean, with their Chair, and with their Advancement office. And they have said, they want BDPA on their campus as well. So we are actively building our college construct by creating college chapters around the country. And we're increasing our portfolio of tech offerings to college students. For example, we're bringing in a new data-science academy, and we're building a cyber-operations apprenticeship program.

Entrepreneurship

Companies are actively seeking to increase the number of black-owned suppliers providing products and services to their organizations. And because BDPA is blessed with an abundance of business-technology resources, and because BDPA has built a 40-year track record of excellence in the information-technology industry, it is not surprising that these companies are coming to BDPA and requesting that we help them identify black-owned tech suppliers who can provide tech products and services to them.

In response to these corporate requests, we are building a supplier-diversity program that will curate a list of black-owned tech-service providers and match that provider list with a list of corporate requests and supplier opportunities. Also, we are going to synchronize this matching service with our apprenticeship and tech-training services for tech students and professionals. So, as we're working through these designs, our hope is to introduce specific plans in the coming months.

Classroom to Boardroom

And one more thing I'll mention is that we're looking to standardize more of our youth programs. In BDPA, we do a lot of good stuff for our young people; like our High School Computer Competition. But we want to standardize our methods around our thirty plus chapters who participate in our youth programs. Standardization will lighten the load on our local chapters, and it will improve the overall quality of our offerings. BDPA's "Classroom to Boardroom" concept is a concept that is broader than building pathways to corporate-boardroom careers. Getting to the boardroom is definitely one of our aims. But more broadly, "Classroom to Boardroom" is also about helping members become outstanding tech specialists, managers, entrepreneurs, and societal contributors in various other capacities.

IT Senior Management Forum (ITSMF)

Specifically as it pertains to helping more of our members obtain senior IT management positions, we are partnering our efforts with the IT Senior Management Forum (ITSMF) organization. As you might already know, ITSMF was founded by members of BDPA, so we've always been friendly. But this year, we reset our partnership with them—and that partnership is growing stronger. We have frequent dialogues to discussing how we can enhance our relationship even more. So we're vested, both of us, because we see the mutual benefit of our working in concert to help black tech professionals obtain senior IT positions of leadership, including boardroom-level jobs.

Our First Virtual National Conference

I count myself fortunate to be helping to lead BDPA through this unique period in history. We were staring at multiple significant challenges last year and this year too; the pandemic being the chief among them.

Last year, one of our most significant challenges is that we were faced with the prospect of having to cancel our national conference. But it just hit me early, that the folks who needed what BDPA was doing the most, would be the folks who would be hurt the most if we cancelled our conference. We felt that it was imperative that we continued doing what we were doing, and we challenged ourselves to do even more—pandemic or no pandemic.

And it was a blessing that we were able to pivot to hosting a virtual national conference on a technology platform that empowered us to be able to offer an amazing conference experience.

Our team did a good job putting it all together. It was our first virtual national conference, but it won't be our last, because we discovered significant cost-saving advantages over doing an in-person conference, plus we discovered some improvements in the overall national conference experience.

Nothing replaces the in-person experience, but it was exciting to discover what could be accomplished online. And so it was a win-win situation, and we have decided to pursue a virtual experience again in 2021; an enhanced experience that will have significantly more sponsors and participants.

Then eventually, after the pandemic is contained, we will reevaluate our global readiness for hosting mass gatherings, and we will take a close look at the pros and cons of hosting an in-person versus a virtual national conference in 2022. So I'm feeling good about how we overcame that obstacle, and I'm feeling really good about our future possibilities.

Help Local Chapters Win

One of the areas that I'm intending to spend more energy on, is strengthening our local BDPA chapters around the country. I mean, we have great people who are passionate about the work they do. But as a volunteer organization, this amazing work that they do is squeezed into the corners of their days and nights, and National BDPA needs to be able to give them more of the help they deserve. So it is my desire that we get back to a paid-staff model where folks can do more of this work during the "eight-to-five" versus the "five-to-eight" timeslots.

I want National BDPA to provide more operational support, so that our local chapter leaders/workers can focus on helping their members, students, and communities, rather than having to focus on operational issues. And my hope is that we can see some measurable progress in providing this help, this year, especially since BDPA is growing again. For example, we expect, in April, to welcome new chapter locations in Monroe Louisiana, and Oklahoma City, Oklahoma.

And we want to improve programs like our "Tech Talk" series, so that we can—more reliably and more consistently—deliver outstanding content-value to our members that is measurable and tweakable over time. And by centralizing the operational issues of delivering programs and content to our members, we can consolidate our resources, and collectively create richer programs that consistently share world-class experiences with our members. And in doing so, we will be able to help more members, and we will be able to engage more corporate support from more organizations like Lilly, who enthusiastically support BDPA's mission.

Help People Move Mountains

Helping others realize their full potential so that they can have full impact, and helping them remove barriers, and helping them think through challenges, is what fuels my fire, and that fire is what gets me up in the morning.

And it was at the 2009 BDPA National Conference in Raleigh, North Carolina (the year I discovered BDPA) where I was exposed to the wisdom of Larry Quinlan, Chief Information Officer (CIO) for Deloitte. And Larry spoke on a panel about having people in the room advocating for you, and you often not knowing that they were doing that. But, you had to have built up the relationship and the credibility with these individuals to get to that level of advocacy. Well, BDPA provides an opportunity to give and receive that advocacy.

And I had the occasion to go to St. Jude's Children's Museum. Danny Thomas (1950s-60s entertainer) was the founder, and it was a massive campus doing great work for children all around the world. And there was a quote that hit me, where Danny was speaking, in 1968. And he said, “If I don't live another moment, I know why I was born.” And that level of fulfillment and self-actualization became my goal. Because when I leave here, I want to have given all I’ve got, and I want to leave it all on the field. And, I feel like the work I’m doing with BDPA, and with my church, is getting me closer to that place where I’m giving all I’ve got. The sky is the limit because the need is so great. The need for BDPA was great in 1975, when the organization was founded, and the need is great in 2021, as we sit here today.

The work we do in BDPA is a movement—not just a moment. We have a long track record of deep passion and expertise in this technology space, and it is our job to educate members and potential partners about what we’ve already accomplished, so that we can help people understand why BDPA is uniquely well positioned to usher in a brighter future.

Kenneth L. Wilson

CHAPTER 15

Kenneth L. Wilson

Co-author of this book, Kenneth L. Wilson is an entrepreneur helping people improve productivity using modern technology. His first business, "Wilco Information Management (Wilco)," thrived for twenty-five years until Ken refocused his efforts building his second company, "Planet Victorious," a nonprofit that publishes "people-bettering" books, including the first three books Ken authored, "*Build a Better You: And Build a Better World,*" "*Planet Victorious: Building a Better World,*" and this one, "*The BDPA Story: How African American Computer Technology Professionals Changed the World.*" Now, in pursuit of finally achieving income and wealth equality for tech professionals, Ken's upcoming book, "*TechOpp,*" describes how the preeminent tech-opportunity network of the 21st Century (TechOpp) is being designed and built using modern technology in a global virtual cloud community. Then the book describes how this network can serve people of all backgrounds in communities across America. According to Ken, the two most important questions we must answer individually and collectively as families, organizations, and nations are, *"Where do we go from here, and why?"* And ultimately, says Ken, all of us are seeking brighter futures.

Creating Pathways to Brighter Futures

By Kenneth L. Wilson

My father was my first role model. Even while others continued to inspire me, my father was the man I wanted to be. Every day, Napoleon Wilson worked hard – and smart. By day, he labored for pay as a hoisting-machine operator at the Grabler Manufacturing Company in Cleveland, Ohio. By night, he labored for love as a commercial artist, painter, and draftsman. His sign-painting business was always in the basement of our home. I grew up loving the smell of turpentine and paint thinner.

During World War II, in Europe, my father surveyed landscapes, sketched maps, and drafted blueprints in the 389th Engineer General Service Regiment, for the United States Army, that built roads and bridges for General Patton's troops.

Sergeant Napoleon Wilson
U.S. Army
World War II
389th Engineer General Service Regiment

When my father returned home after the war ended (before I was born), he completed a degree in Architectural Drafting at the Cleveland Engineering Institute (1949).

Talented, experienced, and educated, Napoleon Wilson carried samples of his artistry and draftsmanship (that helped America win the war against Hitler in Europe) to the employment offices of the Cleveland City Hall, to apply for a job as a Draftsman. Art was his passion. He knew that way back in 1939, when he graduated in Art with honors, from East Technical High School.

Unfortunately, in the post War World II era, in 1949, the City of Cleveland was not hiring "Negroes" as Draftsmen. But what disturbed my father most, (and he shared this with me many times) was that *"They would not even look at my work."* Had they taken even a casual glimpse at his work, they would have known the truth: Napoleon Wilson could have been one of their top Draftsmen.

Undeterred, my father shifted gears and decided to open his own sign painting and drafting business in the basement of our home. The enterprise eventually became "Wilson Signs," and it thrived until 1972, when triumphantly, Napoleon Wilson made a dream deferred come true: His superior talent, impeccable credentials and unswerving persistence finally compelled the City of Cleveland to hire him as a Sign Painter and Draftsman. And then it got even better: How could Napoleon Wilson have possibly known, in

1949, that one day, he would design and produce the official logo for the City of Cleveland Water Department?

Water Department Logo
City of Cleveland
Designed by my father, Napoleon Wilson
1987

That official logo is still proudly displayed on the service trucks of the City of Cleveland Water Department today. Napoleon Wilson's lifetime of achievement is commemorated by the song of triumph, "We Shall Overcome – Some Day."

Ohio Wesleyan University (OWU)

The fact that I would go to college was already decided by my father, mother, and three older sisters, but where I would go was totally up to me. So, after evaluating the four colleges that had extended offers, I chose Ohio Wesleyan University (OWU).

Nestled intimately within OWU's 2000 students were 200 of us (African American students). We were a close-knit community – our own fraternity-sorority – and we celebrated our own culture, comforts, and entertainment. Because, if you wanted to join a Greek fraternity at OWU, you had to, number one, pick a house that welcomed black folks, and number two, you had to agree to act really, really white – like guzzling whole kegs of beer and listening to riotous acid rock, and stuff like that that Black people typically did not do. So, to the University's credit, and because of the arduous work of Pete Smith, Dave Cheever, Stanford Kabir Smith, and other African-American pioneers who came to OWU before us, the university conceded to us "The Black House" and "The Cave."

At "The Cave" on weekends, after classwork, after studying and working our student jobs, we partied like it was 1999. We danced to the musical rhythm and blues and funky grooves of Earth, Wind, and Fire, The Isley Brothers, Kool and the Gang, The Ohio Players, Parliament-Funkadelic, The O'Jays, The Stylistics, The Spinners, The Delfonics, The Commodores, The J.B.'s and more. We had too much fun to tell it all.

The Black House, more appropriately known as "The House of Black Culture," served a different purpose. The House was a residence hall, gathering place, and a cradle of cultural and intellectual exchange. Admittedly, we had fun there too, but we (the brothers and sisters of OWU) were profoundly serious about proactively preparing for our future, our responsibilities, and our cause.

College Dormitory Roommates
Tony Newton, Me, Greg Moore, Greg Davis (L to R)

College Dormitory Roommates

Gregory Moore, my dormitory roommate and best buddy during freshman and sophomore years at OWU, was also from Cleveland – from sports rival

Glenville High School. Greg was inspired to pack two pair of boxing gloves that Greg and I donned occasionally celebrating the close camaraderie of our high-school rivalry with friendly boxing competitions in the dormitory hallways. I won't say who won most of the matches, but changing the subject, Greg always knew he wanted to be a journalist; he nurtured in me a love for writing, and he eventually went on to become Editor in Chief of the Denver Post, and Deke Expert News Engine.

Greg and fellow student Madison King started a Black student newspaper called "The Witness." It helped us appreciate the power of the pen, and was a godsend to our African-American community given that the campus-wide student newspapers, whether intentional or not, treated our concerns as irrelevant or unschooled.

Each one of my roommates were unique, brilliant and wonderful people with whom I had the privilege of sharing interests, ideas, lessons about life and fun. Greg Davis, Mike Ash and Ken Church were my roomies freshman year; Len Birnbach, sophomore year; Greg Moore, freshman and sophomore years; Tony Newton and Mike Hall, senior year. The brotherhood and cultural exchange was amazing.

Computers, Math and Science

My love for science, technology, engineering and mathematics (STEM) had been blooming since 5th grade, so I already knew that the focus of my studies at OWU would be STEM related.

It was during freshman year, that I discovered a brand-new passion – computers – and the student-faculty camaraderie in the computer room became my new home away from home – the parties were only on weekends. On countless occasions, I pulled all-nighters with other geeks and nerds exploring the IBM 1130 and the PDP 11/70. We concocted some remarkable software. For my senior project, under Professor Harold Wiebe, I designed a database prototype for an electronic library-card-catalogue system for Ohio Wesleyan's Beeghly library.

A Typical 1976 Library-Card-Catalogue System
Computers Changed Everything!

In 1976, computers were not what they are today; the Personal Computer (PC) had not yet been invented. Library-card catalogues were composed of hundreds of drawers of manila index cards; organized alphabetically by book-title, and numerically by the Dewey-Decimal book-classification system – like in the photograph above.

Medical School

I originally wanted to be a doctor, so I bombarded myself with every course in biology, chemistry, physics and mathematics that Ohio Wesleyan's Pre-Medicine degree required. Yes, I flunked Organic Chemistry and had to repeat it. But I aced it at Cleveland State in summer school, and all my other science grades were excellent. I got high scores on the Medical College Admissions Test (MCAT), but somehow, I allowed myself to get sidetracked and mesmerized by the lure of immediate dollars.

In one of the most pivotal phone conversations of my life, I turned down an acceptance to attend Medical School. Instead, I opted for a quick payday in the form of a lucrative wage as a computer programmer. In taking the job, I rationalized that I would work for three years, then reapply to medical school after I had earned some quick cash. That decision, THAT DECISION, changed the course of my life, and to this day, I regret bypassing what turned out to be my one and only opportunity to become a medical doctor.

My Computer Programming Career

In 1976, computers had become the heart-throb of business, and programming jobs had become abundant and financially rewarding. And while I was earning a nice paycheck, I had discovered that the job of an entry-level corporate COBOL programmer was dull and mundane compared with what I had envisioned a career in medicine could be. So, I re-applied to medical school one year later, but the doors of admission had slammed shut in my face; My most promising med-school prospect required that I earn a master's degree first to prove "continued interest" and prove "I could handle the work." Sadly, they refused to offer any assurances whatsoever that if I returned with the broomstick of the wicked witch of the west, they would admit me.

Stumbling and Bumbling Forward

Fast forwarding my hobbling programming career to a gloomy day in April 1980: I had been hired by Eaton Corporation (one year earlier in 1979) as a COBOL programmer. I had written over one hundred programs prior, but on this day, I screwed up – not technically, but tactically.

A frustrated pre-med major looking for a new career challenge beyond COBOL programming, my tactical blunder was questioning the applicability of a standard operating procedure that was firmly in place. At the Eaton Telecomputer Center in Eastlake Ohio, it worked like this: Programmers wrote programs, Analysts analyzed systems, and never the twain shall meet – no overlapping duties were allowed.

Certainly, there was nothing wrong with this operating procedure in and of itself, but it constrained me uncomfortably, because number one: I had already, on previous jobs, handled complex analysis assignments, impeccably. And number two: Some of the European-American programmers were getting analysis assignments, contrary to the pretense this procedure was sacred.

On the day of my tactical blunder, I had finished writing my assigned programs way ahead of schedule, and we were short one Analyst for the final phase of the project. The project urgently needed to be completed, and someone urgently needed to meet with the Axle-Division (the old Eaton Axle Division plant on East 140th Street in Cleveland) plant manager, complete the analysis, and write the phase-II system specifications. We were at a standstill until these specifications were completed.

When I suggested to Don, my manager, that I thought it would help the team if I met with the plant manager, I was cut off and castigated, "*You're a programmer. We pay you to program, not to think.*" Maybe Don had bigger problems on his plate that day, and would have responded less antagonistically under different circumstances. But when I heard his actual words above, I took it as an ultimatum to "*Either stay in your* *place, you ungrateful #$@% (It's none of your business we let the white workers have their way. It's a white man's world; get #$@% used to it.), or else gather your things, find the nearest exit, and don't let the door hit you on the way out."*

In earlier conversations with human resources, I was told that the typical wait to be considered for an Analyst job was five years, but the white workers were getting in there after one year. So, once Don pushed my hot button that day, the only question was: Would I quit first, or would they fire me first? Resigned my Eaton career was over, I began looking for a new job. Two weeks later, Don beat me to the punch. I was let go, packed my things, and was escorted to the parking lot.

Circumnavigating race-based obstruction was not my biggest concern as I had learned how to "grin and bear it" in white-centric environments a long time ago. Don just caught me with my guard down that day. My main problem was that COBOL programming was not my ultimate calling. I loved to code, and I was a great coder, but I needed a challenge more closely aligned with what I was put on this earth to do: In pursuit of my ultimate calling, I needed to analyze, design, and build systems – and I needed to build businesses.

Driving home, my 1971 Buick Skylark (Rusty Brown Beauty) was my best friend – They don't build car buddies like they used to. Driving quietly home, *Rusty Brown Beauty* lifted my spirits and whispered, "We'll be back."

Prophetic words! Though at the time, I was clueless about my future: I had no idea that within the next three years, I would launch a thriving business-technology firm (Wilco) that would serve some of the largest companies in Ohio for twenty-five years. Ironically, Eaton Corporation would become one of my best customers. And as if it were already destined for me, building and running businesses would become my strong suit.

My son Kevin and daughter Leslie help me wash my *Rusty Brown Beauty*

THAT DECISION: That same decision that had foiled a promising medical career, had launched an amazing entrepreneurial expedition to the land of ultimate professional fulfillment. Looking back on my childhood, fondly remembering my father; the seeds of entrepreneurship had already been sown.

Help People Win!

Experience has taught me that helping people win is a win-win-win victory. It is a triple-play victory for you, for the person helped, and for the entire planet. When you help someone win, you can't lose. Understandably, some people are reluctant to help others win because they believe that help is like the world's oil supply; that there is a finite supply – and it's costly. People with this view believe that, "The less you get, the more I get," like in the pie-chart below.

A finite view of the "World's Help Supply"

While it is understandable why some people think this way, my view is that the "World Help Supply" more closely resembles the picture on the next page.

A 1944 song says, "You're nobody 'til somebody loves you." And lovingly, I agree. Respectfully, I also suggest: "You're nobody, 'til you help somebody."

Professionally, it is proven, well-established and clear: If you want your business to win, then you must help someone else win.

An infinite view of the "World's Help Supply"

An African-American entrepreneur, father, and family man, my career zig-zagged clumsily after bungling an opportunity to be a doctor and getting fired from a COBOL programming job. I was down, distraught and discouraged.

When you help someone else, you help yourself too.

But that all changed when I started volunteering for a non-profit organization devoted to helping people take on and tackle tech opportunities. My first assignments with the Black Data Processing Associates (BDPA) involved helping form the organization's Cleveland chapter, recruiting new members, launching a local newsletter (Data News), and becoming editor of the organization's national communications publication (The Journal). But the assignment most satisfying of all was mentoring new programmers and helping them find their career paths.

Gratifyingly, helping other programmers overcome their career obstacles was turning out to be easier and more fulfilling than overcoming my own.

Eventually, I became fortified with energy and entrepreneurial insight. And as I continued helping other people win, I continued discovering my own entrepreneurial destiny. And ultimately, I was earning goodwill and favor with people in position to help me.

Simply put: I was living the law of life put forth earlier in this chapter: The best way to win is to first help someone else win.

Norman R. Mays

I was introduced to BDPA by a friend whose leadership example helped me apply in a professional setting what I had long-ago learned in the Bible: Service to others is mandatory and not optional.

In 1979, retired Major Norman R. Mays returned to his hometown, Cleveland, Ohio, and was hired by the Eaton Corporation, at the same location where I was working. That's how we met, and that's how I learned about Norm's plan to launch the third BDPA chapter, in Cleveland.

At lunch, over steak, salad, and soda, Norm shared the BDPA vision and history, and offered me the opportunity of participating in the chapter's formation. And, on Tuesday, January 15, 1980, the Cleveland Chapter of BDPA was born; with Norman Mays as President; Kenneth Russell, VP; Barbara Whitfield, Treasurer; Nadine An-noor, Recording Secretary; and myself, Kenneth Wilson, Membership Communications Coordinator.

When Norm was elected President of the entire national BDPA, the organization grew by leaps and bounds and launched new chapters in fifty U.S. cities within the decade. Currently, Norm is working in the financial services industry.

As there was more than enough work to go around, locally and nationally, BDPA was where I learned to cherish the joy of extreme volunteerism – connecting with people and helping people connect with their careers. A member throughout BDPA Cleveland Chapter's entire 40-year history, I have enjoyed serving the organization more than 35 of those 40 years, including eight years as Cleveland Chapter President.

My BDPA buddies abound, but I would be remiss if I did not mention the handful of BDPA members who, without them, my life would be incomplete: Sandra Noble, David Ford, Vivian Wilson (resting in peace), Hank Lawson, Henry Ford (resting in peace), Gerry McClamy, Bill Darling, Kelvie Tyus, and of course Norman Mays. Former National President Vivian C. Wilson was a "mover and a shaker" who was amazingly instrumental in BDPA's phenomenal growth.

Looking back, time flies when you're having fun and making a difference in people's lives. Forty years have come and gone, but I still enjoy working with BDPA and several other great community organizations. Over the years, I've worked with BDPA, Career Beginnings, Youth Opportunities Unlimited, Junior Achievement, Boy Scouts of America, Inroads, National Black MBA Association, and the Urban League. Oh yeah: Coaching community league baseball and basketball teams, and teaching Sunday School to teenagers at my church has taught me a lot too.

I learned that the advantages of helping people are too good to pass up. Even when I miss out on an opportunity or two, I still know that the benefits of giving are shared equally; between the giver and the receiver. Yes! Living day-to-day, helping people can be hard and seemingly thankless work. But on a higher plane, being an agent for someone's success is an honor, privilege, and blessing.

Find Your Forté

After leaving Eaton Corporation in 1980 (See Above), I was elated to land a position at Cleveland State University (CSU). The people at the university were great, and the idea of working for a college had always appealed to me. I was assigned to a team developing a university-financial-accounting system using a database technology called Integrated Database Management Store (IDMS). The technology had captured a huge following in companies in the Cleveland, Akron, and Canton Ohio areas. This huge following was partly because IDMS was originally developed by the B.F. Goodrich Company in Akron, Ohio in the 1960s. That was back when Akron, Ohio was the tire-manufacturing capital of the world: Akron headquartered Goodyear, Firestone, and B.F. Goodrich, in addition to dozens of other tire-related manufacturers.

The database technology enthralled me, and I quickly became the IDMS-database "go-to" person on the project, and for the entire Computer-Services department at Cleveland State.

We had just completed the financial-accounting system project when I was approached by a business-technology-consulting company named *Creative*

Computing – they were looking for IDMS talent. And when *Creative* offered to double my salary, I reluctantly resigned from Cleveland State and became a *Creative Consultant*. In a business-technology-consulting firm, a consultant was assigned to a customer on a project-by-project basis. My second assignment with *Creative* was to be the first consultant assigned to *Creative's* new client, The Babcock & Wilcox Company (B&W), in Barberton, Ohio. By 1983, I had become one of Northeast, Ohio's leading practitioners and instructors of the Integrated Database Management Store (IDMS), and my job at B&W was to teach, lead, and mentor the project team implementing a new marketing information system. This undertaking was vast and complex, but my father had taught me to "keep it simple," so I decided that my initial objective going into the project would be: Memorize everybody's name (40 people), learn something significant about each person, what they desired – and discover more comprehensively, what Babcock & Wilcox actually needed. President Theodore Roosevelt said it best, "Nobody cares how much you know, until they know how much you care."

Having accomplished my above-mentioned customer-rapport-building objective in the first week, I began working closely with the B&W managers and staff; teaching the IDMS technology and completing the project plans. One month later, the project plans were completed, and three additional *Creative* consultants joined me at B&W. The Marketing Information System (MKIS) project progressed so smoothly, that *Creative* was awarded several additional projects.

One year later, I was falling more deeply in love with life in this world of information-technology, consulting, marketing, and customer-service. Upon reflection, the only piece missing from a perfect-puzzle was business ownership. So, in 1984, I decided to follow my heart, and venture out on my own. Wilco Information Management, Inc. (Wilco) was born.

Having found my forté, it was immensely helpful that I was an active volunteer in a business-technology association called BDPA. One of BDPA's members, Sandra Noble, was a Project Manager for a management-consulting firm called Anacomp (Anacomp was later acquired by Electronic Data Services (EDS). Remember Ross Perot?). Sandra was responsible for hiring consultants for her project, and fortunately, having worked for Sandra a few years before, she already knew that I had the talent to accomplish everything that was needed. For these reasons, Anacomp became Wilco's first customer. As the Anacomp project progressed, I was approached by the Independent Computer Consultants Association (ICCA) to put together a workshop to teach its members IDMS database technology. The workshops were so well received, that I developed a *Wilco* series of IDMS workshops that were (also) so well received, that I decided to focus the entire company on serving IDMS customers. Pretty soon, the phones were ringing off the hook with calls from Progressive Insurance, Glidden Paints,

General Electric, BP Oil, Dow Chemical, and eventually Eaton Corporation. Because of a decline in the American Automobile Components industry in the late 1970s, Eaton Corporation had engaged in an aggressive diversification strategy. I vividly remember the Cutler-Hammer acquisition that put Eaton in the electronics industry because I was employed at Eaton when it was completed in 1979. Cutler-Hammer was the largest acquisition in Eaton's history up until that point, and Eaton continued its growth-by-acquisition strategy into the 1990s. The strategy necessitated that Eaton hire short-term-contract consultants; hence Eaton was looking for technology-consulting firms that understood its business. In 1993, Eaton called on Wilco, Wilco answered the call, and Eaton remained a satisfied Wilco client for the next fifteen years.

Wilco Home Office
Technology Education Center Entrance

Technology Education Center

Times and techniques were changing, and by 1993, a brand new "relational database" technology had emerged. To keep pace, companies began moving their systems from IDMS to new state-of-the-art relational-database-management products by IBM (DB2), Microsoft (SQL), and Oracle (Oracle).

With the future in mind, Wilco had already started its migration to the new technologies in 1989. So, when companies began to call for Oracle expertise, Wilco answered those calls.

Most notably, when Eaton launched its worldwide conversion to Oracle in 1996, Wilco's Technology Education Center provided the *Introduction to Oracle* classes.

Wilco Technology Education Center - 1996

Continued Success

For the next several years, Wilco maintained steady growth, and the Wilco Technology Education Center expanded to provide business-technology training and consulting to major corporations in Ohio, Kentucky, Pennsylvania, Indiana, and Illinois. To our popular series of successful Oracle seminars, we added business intelligence and data-analytics symposiums. Back in 1997, when I met Oracle Chairman Larry Ellison in Los Angeles at an Oracle-Business-Partner conference, our Oracle training and consulting business had taken off like a rocket ship.

The Great Recession of 2008 hit me hard, but eventually, those things I did right (like helping other people succeed first) became exactly what I started doing again. And lo and behold: Not only did God grant me a better business, but God also granted me, during my wilderness experiences, a better me, and God granted me a vision of a better world; thank God for the hurdles placed in my path because now I jump higher.

We are reborn every morn' the sun comes up, and no matter how down, destroyed, or distraught we may feel, God has already granted exoneration, rejuvenation, and a brand-new start. Best of all, this gift of God is available to all 7.5 billion human souls living on planet Earth. Because, when you get right down to it, all 7.5 billion of us are kindred souls, and the fates and fortunes of you, your business and our planet are indivisibly interconnected.

Planet Victorious

Planet Victorious is my non-profit organization whose mission was inspired by my book of the same name. Through the Planet Victorious organization, I publish books and offer "thought leadership" about how we can build a world that is better than the one we live in today. Consider, for example, my envisionings on "Global Community."

Global Community

Imagine a global community; a world pursuing a morally upright and honorable future; a community building a thriving free enterprise on a just and equitable global foundation; providing food, water and shelter for every global citizen; demanding equal opportunity for everyone to work and earn these necessities; with good health, clean energy and conservation, resulting in a life-

sustainable planet; building a vibrant Science, Technology, Engineering, and Mathematics (STEM) workforce; utilizing high-impact-low-cost learning, mentoring and partnering; a world where people of all backgrounds become world-class workers; builders of a better humankind; a team of global citizens; working together and achieving this consecrated calling; learning from history, rebuilding mutual trust, and restoring our faith; doing what really needs to get done; cutting out the greed, and cutting out the crap; embracing a new industrial reawakening; always building what's morally upright, honorable and uplifting for our global community.

Imagining the Impossible

Imaginations energize our hope for a brighter tomorrow. They make us strive to achieve utopian aims, like the aforementioned global community first introduced in my 2017 book, "Planet Victorious: Building a Better World." Okay, I'll admit that building this global community is more than a Mount Everest climb. And some might say, "It's impossible. It's undoable." And for emphasis, they might add, "And anybody who thinks otherwise needs to have their head examined." Well, this would not be the first time I've been accused of needing my head examined. But I say what the great Nelson Mandela said, "It always seems impossible until it's done." And Mr. Mandela inspires me to add, "Without vision, the impossible would never get done." Fire would never have been industrialized. Man would never have flown. South Africa would never have been freed. Occasionally therefore, the impossible <u>does</u> get done. And way more often than occasionally, big goals <u>do</u> get achieved.

Nelson Mandela – The Great Humanitarian

Inspired by our founder's bold imaginings, BDPA has achieved the impossible over and over again. We are loaded with talented and hard-working tech professionals who help businesses, students, and communities; that has a lot to do with our success. Our talent pool, knowledge base, and programs are outstanding; that's another reason why we've done so well. And while we're talking about doing the impossible, BDPA accomplishes more than organizations with ten times our program funding and marketing resources.

Creating Pathways to Brighter Futures

Ever since BDPA was founded in 1975, we have formed teams of BDPA members that build people up, and knock barriers down. We don't let hard work get in our way because building IT careers, mentoring students, and uplifting our community is a labor of love we cherish. We continually strive to do great things. In pursuit of this excellence, we often succeed. But whether we succeed or need to try again, we always strive to do what's right.

BDPA has overcome greater challenges than those facing us today. But as times change, so must BDPA.

Our success should not be measured by how well we keep on doing the same old thing. Rather our success should be measured by how well we clear pathways for future growth and for future generations to travel.

And if we're doing our jobs, they will travel beyond destinations we could, just a few years ago, not even imagine. As the savvy tech leader in the illustration below has just discovered: Construction is already underway. Tomorrow is being built by BDPA today.

Founder's Closing Remarks

Earl A. Pace, Jr.

FOUNDER'S CLOSING REMARKS

Earl A. Pace, Jr.

Depending upon how quickly this book gets to publication, if you are reading this portion I may have already passed on. I am suffering from an illness called Amyloidosis; which is a genetic disease that causes secretion of a sticky protein that attaches itself to other body tissues and keeps them from functioning properly. It is prevalent in African American males and normally is hereditary, at least my case. I urge the reader, should they fall into the category of a person of color, that they get checked for Amyloidosis. It is difficult to detect and in some cases doctors cannot diagnose it, but as in my case, it is fatal.

As you have read, BDPA has a rich history through five decades and we are very proud of that, However, it hasn't always been peaches and cream. In most organizations—and BDPA is no exception—there are times when decisions do not work out as intended.

Nonetheless, when these organizational missteps happen, having good leadership, processes, and "checks and balances" already in place is essential.

BDPA has had its share of what some would consider "not quite so good decisions." However, it is a testament to our depth of leadership and our unwavering commitment to BDPA's vision that we have kept our BDPA ship "afloat, on course," and effective for more than 45 years.

When one thinks about it, it's amazing what we might have achieved had we received more robust financial support during our early years. Yet today we are more optimistic as we see the tide turning, particularly after the last four years. We are seeing more and more corporate representation and sponsorship and we expect that there will be even more as the future holds great promise and potential for all of us.

BDPA is great because BDPA changed the world. Before BDPA, blacks in technology had been pushed to the back of the employment line. But after BDPA started in 1975, we started finding employment with our computer technology skills. And today, we are way ahead of where we would have been had it not been for BDPA.

I want to thank each of the interviewees who have taken the time to share their personal stories – which are a reflection of each of us. I also want to thank the organizations that have helped us along the way and those that are still with us today. Special thanks go out to the current award winning members and chapters, and especially to all of the students who have participated in our various training and mentoring programs.

As we move into a new era of opportunity in technology, the telling of our story should be seen as a new era of opportunity in BDPA. I encourage new authors to step up and continue to tell the ongoing story of BDPA. The technologies that we helped to create and perfect have melded into fantastic realities, such as Artificial Intelligence (AI), The Internet of Things (IOT), and Robotics—all blending into applications like space travel, NASA interstellar probes, and the MARS Rover.

Our future can be even brighter when we follow the examples of great Americans like former NASA astronaut, Dr. Mae Jemison (in the photograph above). Dr. Jemison graduated from Stanford University with degrees in chemical engineering and African-American studies. She then earned her medical degree from Cornell University. Jemison was a doctor for the Peace Corps in Liberia and Sierra Leone from 1983 until 1985 and worked as a general practitioner. In pursuit of becoming an astronaut, she applied to NASA, and in 1992 Astronaut Mae Jemison became the first African American woman to travel into space as a mission specialist aboard the Space Shuttle Endeavour. In her keynote address at the 2004 National BDPA Conference in Dallas, Texas, Dr. Jemison inspired us to "reach for the stars," and she shared, "I had to learn very early not to limit myself due to others' limited imaginations." I agree wholeheartedly, moreover, we must not allow others' limited expectations of us stifle our greatness.

Looking forward to the year 2025 and the celebration of BDPA's 50th Anniversary, I trust that all future organizational decisions will be made with sound judgment, good intentions and within the policies, bylaws and guidelines of our organization. My experiences in business and BDPA have taught me a lot, and in closing, I'll share three of the most essential leadership lessons I've learned.

Lesson 1: Keep the organization focused on our mission and vision while moving toward achieving them. As I stated in Chapter One, "To me, the end goal is *economic parity*," for our members, our careers, and our communities;

Lesson 2: Ensure that we have processes in place to consistently and accurately oversee fiscal obligations. In all business activities, define roles, responsibilities, and accountabilities. And;

Lesson 3: Continue nurturing our BDPA-family environment of mentoring, coaching and recognizing the accomplishments of all members—students, seasoned professionals, and all who support our amazing mission. Then, after all is said and done, relax, have fun, and enjoy life.

As BDPA moves to a new administration, the transfer to a new national president offers another opportunity for BDPA to rise to new heights. Many thanks to Mr. Terry Morris for his service as national president. With great leaders like Terry, incoming President Tim Brown, and other future BDPA leaders, who knows; maybe the heavens aren't limits, but are milestones towards unimaginable universal achievements. Stay tuned...!!! Together, WE ARE BDPA.

Thank you for the opportunity to be recognized as Co-Founder of such a significant organization as BDPA. I hope I have not disappointed anyone.

May Jehovah bless each of you!

Earl A. Pace, Jr.
Co-Founder
Black Data Processing Associates (BDPA)
December 31, 2021

Appendices

A. BDPA Chapters

B. National Presidents

C. National Conferences

D. BDPA Programs

E. Technology Timeline

Appendix A

BDPA Chapters

BDPA CHAPTERS

February 2022

MIDWEST	NORTHEAST	SOUTH	WEST
Central Illinois	Baltimore	Atlanta	Austin
Chicago	Boston MetroWest	Baton Rouge	Bay Area
Cincinnati	Hartford	Charlotte	Dallas
Cleveland	New Jersey	Birmingham	Houston
Detroit	New York	Huntsville	Los Angeles
Indianapolis	N. Deleware	Memphis	Nevada
Kansas City	N. Virginia	Mid Tennessee	Oklahoma City
Milwaukee	Philadelphia	Monroe	Seattle
S. Minnesota	Rhode Island	Richmond	
St. Louis	Washington, D.C.	S. Florida	
Twin Cities		Triangle	

Appendix B

National Presidents

Eight National Presidents on One Stage

Denise Holland, Gina Billings, Milt Haynes, George Williams Diane Davis, Vivian Wilson, Norman Mays, Earl Pace (L to R).

Terry Morris, National President 2018-2021

BDPA NATIONAL PRESIDENTS

#	NAME	YEARS IN OFFICE
1	Earl Pace	1976-1980
2	Norman Mays	1981-1984
3	Gerard Anderson	1985-1988
4	Vivian Wilson	1989-1992
5	Dianne Davis	1993-1994
6	Ollie Morgan	1995-1995
7	George Williams	1995-1999
8	Renee McClure	1999-2001
9	Milt Haynes	2002-2003
10	Wayne Hicks	2004-2005
11	Gina Billings	2006-2007
12	Denise Holland	2008-2009
13	Yvette Graham	2010-2011
14	Monique Berry	2012-2013
15	Craig Brown	2014-2015
16	Pamela Matthews	2015-2016
17	Mike Williams	2016-2017
18	Terry Morris	2018-2021
19	Tim Brown	2022-

Appendix C

National Conferences

COX
8
BDPA
ogle

YEAR	NATIONAL CONFERENCE THEME	CITY
2021	Powered Together - A Revolution of Excellence	Virtual Conference
2020	vBDPACON2020	Virtual Conference
2019	BDPA 2019	Atlanta. Georgia
2018	BDPA 2018 – Experience the Future Now!	New Orleans, LA
2017	BDPA Disrupt 2017	Cincinnati, OH
2016	BDPA Connect 2016	Atlanta, GA
2015	40TH ANNIVERSARY- The evolution of I.T.	Washington, DC
2014	Race to Innovate	Indianapolis, IN
2013	Diverse Opportunities in the Age of Convergence	Washington, DC
2012	Ignite, Inspire & Empower: The GPS of Future Technologists	Chicago, IL
2011	Transforming the IT Professional	Baltimore, MD
2010	Access for All	Philadelphia, PA
2009	Challenges for Today – Strategies for Tomorrow	Raleigh, NC
2008	Harnessing Emerging Technologies to Advance IT Careers	Atlanta, GA
2007	Global Strategy for the IT Professional	Washington, DC
2006	Picturing the Future of Information Technology	Los Angeles, CA
2005	Driving Innovation, Bringing Value and Embracing Change	Detroit, MI
2004	BDPA: Securing Our Future Through Technology	Dallas, TX
2003	Information Technology: From Classroom to Boardroom	Philadelphia, PA
2002	Changing the Culture of IT: From Access to Ownership	Orlando, FL
2001	Empowering the Nation Through Information	Chicago, IL

Conference Career Fair Participants

BDPA 2020 Virtual Conference

Due to the global pandemic, BDPA conferences were virtual in both 2020 and 2021.

YEAR	NATIONAL CONFERENCE THEME	CITY
2000	Taking IT to the Net: From High-Tops to High-Tech	Washington, DC
1999	Closing the Gap in Information Technology	Atlanta, GA
1998	Unveiling the Magic of Emerging Technologies	Orlando, FL
1997	Looking at Tomorrow, Today	Houston, TX
1996	Building World Class Skills for Information Technology	Atlanta, GA
1995	Linking Business, Education and Technology	Philadelphia, PA
1994	Unleashing the Power of a Creative People	Cleveland, OH
1993	Cultivating Tomorrow's Leaders in the Heart of America	Kansas City, OH
1992	Shaping the Information Technology Professional	Detroit, MI
1991	BDPA Getting to the Core of Technology	New York, NY
1990	Education and Technology Bonding for Excellence	Washington, DC
1989	Ideas in the Making	Los Angeles, CA
1988	Growth and Success by Design	Chicago, IL
1987	A Bridge to Success	New Orleans, LA
1986	Securing Your Professional Future	Atlanta, GA
1985	A Decade of Professional Growth	Philadelphia, PA
1984	Information Processing: A Vote for the Future	Cleveland, OH
1983	Rise to the Challenge	Newark, NJ
1982	Entrepreneurship: A Successful Attitude	Detroit, MI
1981	Growth Through Professional Association	Philadelphia, PA
1980	A New Era of Minority Involvement in Data Processing	Washington, DC
1979	The Role of the Black Technical Organization	Washington, DC

Appendix D

BDPA Programs

BDPA Programs

BDPA offers a variety of programs for Information Technology (IT) Professionals, Students, and Entrepreneurs. These programs are listed on the next page:

Students Learn in Youth Technology Camp

Students Focus in Computer Competition

IT Professional Development

- BDPA IT Institute, featuring professional IT certifications and discounted courses
- National BDPA Technology Conference, featuring professional workshops & seminars
- Information Technology Senior Management Forum (ITSMF)
- Executive Leadership Program
- Leadership & Career Development Webinars
- National BDPA Career Center and Talent Management System
- Local Chapter Professional Development Programs
- Job Seekers Forum
- Entrepreneur Advisory Group

Student Programs

- Student Information Technology Education & Scholarship (SITES) training programs
- Youth Technology Camp (YTC)
- National High School Computer Competition (HSCC)
- Awards, Scholarships, and Tablets for Teens
- Information Technology (IT) Showcase
- Information Technology (IT) Corps
- HSCC Alumni Program
- College Student Internship Program (SIP)
- College Mentoring Program

Appendix E

Technology Timeline

Mary W. Jackson

Human Computer - Mary W. Jackson 1951

Mary W. Jackson started as a "Computer" at the segregated West Area Computing division in 1951. She took advanced engineering classes and, in 1958, became NASA's first black female engineer. Mary W. Jackson is a technology hero. Her story is featured in the book and movie *Hidden Figures*. Ms. Jackson was a mathematician and aerospace engineer at the National Aeronautics and Space Administration (NASA). She worked at Langley Research Center in Hampton, Virginia for most of her career. The word "Computer" was originally a job title for professionals who used mathematics, science, and their brain to perform complex computations.

Keyboard Input to Computers 1951

Before 1951, computer users fed their programs into a computer using console switches, punched cards or paper tape. Then, researchers began experimenting with direct keyboard input to computers, today´s normal mode of operation. An experiment conducted on the MIT Whirlwind computer confirmed how useful and convenient a keyboard input device could be. Joe Thompson (in the photograph on the next page) was one of the first Whirlwind operators in 1951.

Digital Equipment Corp. Founded 1957

Digital Equipment Corporation (DEC) was co-founded by Ken Olsen and Harlan Anderson in 1957 to, initially, make electronic modules for test, measurement, prototyping and control markets. Digital Equipment Corporation was headquartered in Maynard, Massachusetts.

Joe Thompson at Direct Keyboard Input Computer 1951

COBOL Programming Language 1959

COBOL—an acronym for "Common Business-Oriented Language"—was developed in 1959, and was based on the earlier FLOW-MATIC language designed by Grace Hopper. An American computer scientist and United States Navy Rear Admiral, Grace Hopper was the first to devise the theory of machine-independent programming languages—a concept so big that a woman in 1959 could not have possibly come up with it. But somehow, she did. The FLOW-MATIC programming language she created using this concept was later extended to create the COBOL programming language, an early high-level programming language still in use today. COBOL was less cryptic than other languages because it resembled the English language.

Timesharing Online Communities 1961

By the early 1960s many people can share a single computer, using teletype terminals, modems, and phone lines connected to the single computer. They were called timesharing computers because many users shared time on one computer. Several companies, known as "Service Bureaus," started providing timesharing services for a fee.

ASCII 1963

ASCII — American Standard Code for Information Interchange — permits machines from different manufacturers to exchange data. ASCII codes, developed from telegraph code, represent text in computers, telecommunications equipment, and other devices. The standardization of these codes enabled any device to communicate with any other device using the ASCII standard.

Grace Hopper invented COBOL

Apollo Guidance Computer 1968

Designed by scientists and engineers at MIT's Instrumentation Laboratory, the Apollo Guidance Computer (AGC) is the culmination of years of work to reduce the size of the Apollo spacecraft computer from the size of seven refrigerators side-by-side to a compact unit weighing only 70 lbs. and taking up a volume of less than 1 cubic foot. The AGC's first flight was on Apollo 7. A year later, it steered Apollo 11 to the lunar surface.

Networks Go Online 1969

Switched on in late October 1969, the ARPAnet is the first large-scale, general-purpose computer network to connect different kinds of computers together.

C Programming Language 1972

The C programming language was created at Bell Laboratories by Dennis Ritchie and his team, and they soon thereafter rewrote the source code for Unix in C. As a result, Unix was easily ported to other computers and Unix spread quickly. The C programming language is still widely used today.

Ethernet and Local Networks 1973

Ethernet is a family of wired computer technologies commonly used in local area networks. Developed at Xerox PARC between 1973 and 1974, Ethernet initially competed with Token Ring and other communication protocols. Over time, the Ethernet standard prevailed, and like other standard protocols that eventually prevailed, Ethernet got everybody speaking the same language.

The Apple II Computer

BDPA is Launched 1975

Earl A. Pace, Jr. and David Wimberly launch BPDA in Philadelphia in 1975. A few years later, Earl Pace, Wilbur McReynolds, Ralph Gordon, and Norman Mays (left to right in the photo), reorganized BDPA into a national organization with chapters in Philadelphia, Washington, D.C., and Cleveland.

CP/M is Developed 1976

CP/M computers became an early standard in the microcomputer industry that was widely used in business through the late 1970s. CP/M developer Digital Research was approached by IBM about providing an operating system for its PC. But Microsoft won the two-horse competition with its own operating system; MS-DOS.

Apple II Introduced 1977

Before the Apple-II, Apple computer users were hobbyists—almost exclusively. But the Apple-II became the world's first highly successful mass-produced microcomputer product because the brilliant graphics it produced, when connected to a color television set, made it popular in American households.

The DEC VAX Introduced 1978

The Digital Equipment Corporation (DEC) VAX computers rivaled much more expensive mainframe computers in performance and features. The name "VAX" is an acronym for *Virtual Address eXtension*, because the VAX was a 32-bit extension of the older 16-bit PDP-11, and because it used virtual memory. DEC was the leading maker of mini-computers.

IBM Personal Computer (PC)

WordStar is Created 1978

WordStar is a word processor application for personal computers that dominated the market in the early and mid-1980s. It was published by MicroPro International, originally written for CP/M, and later written also for MS-DOS.

VisiCalc is Created 1979

VisiCalc was the first spreadsheet application for personal computers. Introduced by VisiCorp, it is the app that turned the PC from a hobby toy into a business tool, prompting IBM to introduce its PC.

IBM Personal Computer (PC) 1981

The IBM PC revolutionized business computing by becoming the first PC to gain widespread adoption by industry. Released on August 12, 1981, the only significant business industry competition it faced was from the Apple Macintosh.

MS-DOS Released with the IBM PC 1981

MS-DOS (the Microsoft Disk Operating System) was the basic software for the IBM PC, and kicked off the start of a partnership between IBM and Microsoft—the startup founded by Bill Gates and Paul Allen six years earlier. IBM's PC inspired hardware imitators, but for software, most manufacturers licensed MS-DOS.

Lotus 1-2-3 1982

Mitch Kapor developed Lotus 1-2-3, a software suite for the IBM PC that combined a word processor, spreadsheet, and database.

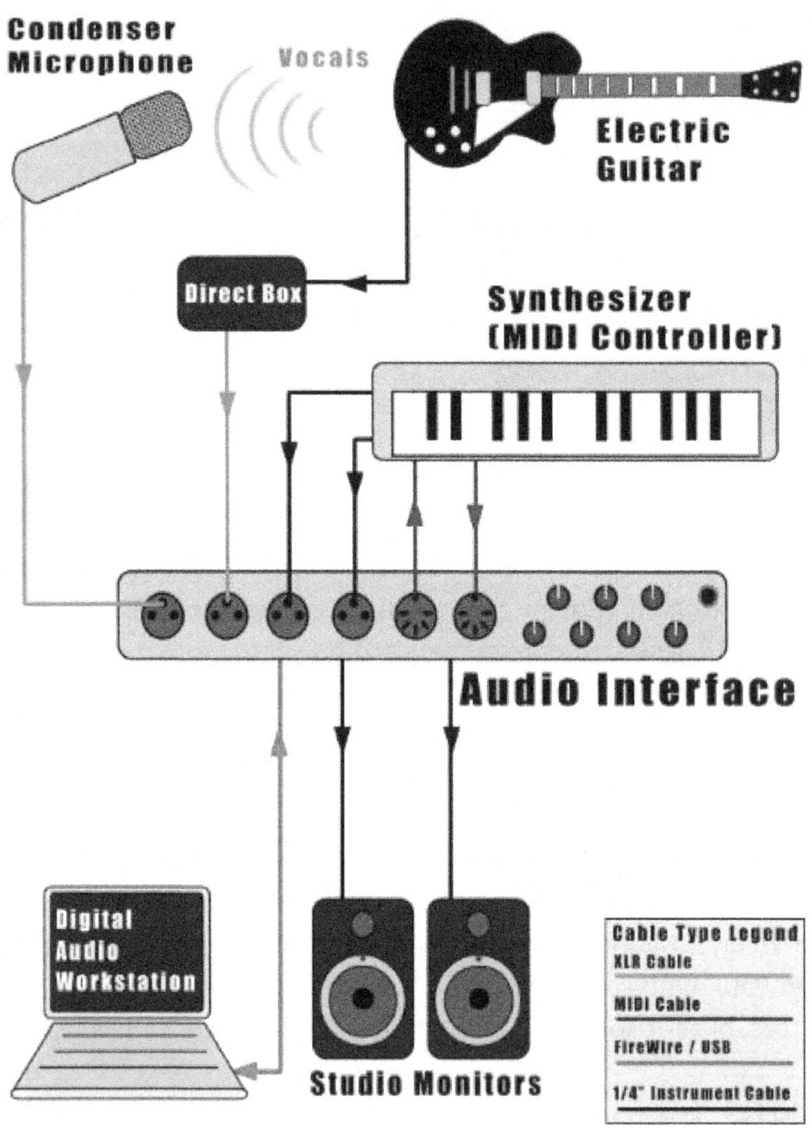

The MIDI Musical Interface

The Commodore 64 Introduced 1982

The Commodore 64 was introduced in January 1982. It sold for $595, came with 64 KB of RAM, featured impressive graphics, and was one of the highest selling computer models of all time. Thousands of software titles were released over its lifespan, and by the time it was discontinued in 1993, it had sold more than 22 million units.

CD-ROM 1983

The Compact Disk — Read Only Memory (CD-ROM) was able to hold 550 megabytes of pre-recorded data. It was created based on the designs of music Compact Disks (CDs). Music CDs, for distributing music, were developed by Sony and Philips in 1982. The entire 9 million words in the *Grolier´s Electronic Encyclopedia* took up only 12 percent of the available space.

The MIDI Musical Interface 1983

The Musical Instrument Digital Interface (MIDI) is a technical standard that describes a communications protocol, digital interface, and electrical connectors that connect a wide variety of electronic musical instruments, computers, and related audio devices for playing, editing, and recording music.

Microsoft Introduces Word 1983

Microsoft Word competed with WordPerfect for market share as a word processing program, and it was not until Word for Windows was introduced in 1989 that it became a global standard. Over time, it pushed WordPerfect out of the mainstream and into only a few niche industries—law firms most notably.

Dr. Jesse Bemley

Apple Launches the Macintosh 1984

The first Macintosh was introduced on January 24, 1984, by Steve Jobs and it was the first commercially successful PC to feature a "mouse," and a "graphical user interface (GUI)," rather than the "command-line interface" of its predecessors. Based on the Motorola 68000 microprocessor, the Apple Macintosh was priced at $2,500.

High School Computer Competition 1986

Dr. Jesse Bemley launched the BDPA High School Computer Competition at the 1986 National BDPA Conference in Atlanta, Georgia. What started as a two-team event launched a revolution that has groomed thousands of computer tech professionals. BDPA's competition idea has been imitated across America.

The World Wide Web is Launched 1989

Tim Berners-Lee invented the World Wide Web (WWW) in 1989, while working at CERN. The Web was originally conceived and developed to meet the demand for automated information-sharing between scientists in universities and institutes around the world. By Christmas 1990, he had prototyped a World Wide Web, featuring a server, HTML, URLs, and the first browser.

Microsoft Windows NT is Released 1990

Microsoft Windows NT was the first truly 32-bit version of Windows from Microsoft. The increased speed of the 32-bit system made it appealing to high-end engineering and scientific users that required better performance. Several subsequent versions of Windows were based on NT technology.

Java™

Java 1.0 is Introduced 1995

Java is a general-purpose programming language intended to let application developers "write once, run anywhere (WORA)," meaning that compiled Java code can run on all platforms that support Java without the need for recompilation.

Sony Releases PlayStation 1995

The Sony PlayStation was released worldwide in 1995. Sony and console manufacturer Nintendo collaborated to create the PlayStation, a CD-ROM-based version of the Super Nintendo gaming system. The PlayStation was a huge success, and Sony became a dominant participant in the home gaming market. It's successor, the PlayStation 2 (released in 2000) is the bestselling home game console of all time.

Microsoft Introduces Visual Studio 1997

Microsoft Visual Studio is an integrated development environment (IDE) developed by Microsoft. It is used to develop computer programs, websites, web apps, and mobile apps. The first version was released in 1997. The idea of visual programming is to let programmers develop software using built-in visual elements instead of text only.

Wi-Fi Comes Home 1999

The growing IEEE 802.11b short-range radio networking standard was re-branded "Wi-Fi" by the Wi-Fi Alliance in 1999. This re-branding (and other consumer products) help popularize cable-free connections to networks at work, in cafes, and at home.

David L. Steward — World Wide Technology Founder

USB Flash Drive 2000

A USB flash drive includes flash memory and an integrated USB interface. Often referred to as a jump drive or memory stick, its portability, re-writability and capacity led to its popularity.

World Wide Technology Hits a Billion 2003

In 1990, David L. Steward founded World Wide Technology, Inc. (WWT), one of the largest African-American-owned businesses in America. In 2003, WWT revenues passed $1 billion, and in 2018, revenues exceeded $11 billion. Mr. Steward, one of 20 black billionaires worldwide, has participated in several BDPA events, most recently at the 2020 national conference.

The Human Genome Project 2003

Completed in April 2003, the Human Genome Project gave us the ability, for the first time, to read nature's complete genetic blueprint for building a human being. The whole project involved information acquisition, processing, and storage, and high-speed computers made that possible. Computers uncover matches in DNA sequences that served to unravel the code.

Amazon Web Services 2006

Amazon Web Services (AWS), a subsidiary of Amazon, provides on-demand cloud computing platforms and APIs to individuals, companies, and governments on a pay-as-you-go basis. Use of the on-demand cloud eliminates the need for a company to purchase and maintain expensive and complex computing infrastructure. AWS was first introduced in 2006.

Apple iPhone

The Apple iPhone is Released 2007

First released in 2007, the Apple iPhone is a web browser, music player and cell phone (combined) that can download added functionality in the form of "apps" (applications) from the online Apple store. The touchscreen smartphone also has built-in GPS navigation, high-definition camera, texting, and more.

Bitcoin 2008

On August 18, 2008, the domain name bitcoin.org was registered, and that same year, Satoshi Nakamoto published *Bitcoin: A Peer-to-Peer Electronic Cash System*, describing the use of peer-to-peer networks to generate a "crypto-currency." In the Bitcoin system, users run software that searches for blocks of data, the discovery of which rewards the users with Bitcoins.

The Mobile Web 2009

Traditionally, the World Wide Web had been access via fixed-line services on laptops and desktop computers. The iPhone's phenomenal popularity created a new computing platform that delivered mobile Web browsing to a larger audience. Google's Android mobile platform soon made that audience even larger.

Artificial Intelligence Wins Jeopardy 2010

In 2010, the IBM Watson artificial intelligence (AI) computer competed against former *Jeopardy!* Tournament of Champion contestants and finished with a 71% winning percentage. This was a prelude for a 2011 matchup where Watson would beat two former human *Jeopardy!* champions. AI had finally arrived.

Dr. Kizzmekia Corbett developed COVID-19 Vaccine

Arab Spring Social Media Protests 2011

Starting in the spring of 2011, protests in several largely Muslim countries (including Tunisia, Morocco, Syria, Libya, Egypt and Bahrain) led to regime change, and for some, free elections for the first time in history. Many of these protests were organized or promoted on sites such as Twitter and Facebook.

SIRI is Announced 2011

Siri was introduced as a feature built in with the Apple iPhone 4S smartphone in October 2011. A voice-activated virtual assistant, Siri could "hear" natural language requests and adjust information it pulled from the internet by learning a user's tendencies and preferences. Returned results are individualized.

Driverless Transportation 2016

On April 7, 2016, a convoy of self-driving trucks completed the world's first European cross-border trip. Computer AI on the job.

COVID-19 Vaccine 2021

Dr. Kizzmekia S. Corbett was instrumental in groundbreaking research that directly led to development of the Moderna COVID-19 vaccine. A viral immunologist, Dr. Corbett is assistant professor of immunology and infectious diseases at the Harvard University School of Public Health, and was highlighted in the *Time's* "Time100 Next" list under the category of innovators. Not long ago, The first sequencing of virus pathogens would take over a year to do. Now, thanks to software, high-speed computers, and scientists like Dr. Corbett, it can be done in one day.

"Service to others is the rent you pay for your room here on earth."

—Muhammad Ali

Made in United States
Orlando, FL
20 July 2022